THE VENICE LETTERS

By the same author

STORIES TOTO TOLD ME
IN HIS OWN IMAGE
CHRONICLES OF THE HOUSE OF BORGIA
HADRIAN THE SEVENTH
DON TARQUINIO
THE WEIRD OF THE WANDERER
THE DESIRE AND PURSUIT OF THE WHOLE
HUBERT'S ARTHUR
NICHOLAS CRABBE
DON RENATO
COLLECTED POEMS
THE ARMED HANDS

FR ROLFE
BARON CORVO

The Venice Letters

EDITED AND
WITH AN INTRODUCTION BY
CECIL WOOLF

1974
CECIL & AMELIA WOOLF
LONDON

Copyright © 1974 by Cecil Woolf
Published by Cecil & Amelia Woolf
Kingly Court, 10 Kingly Street, London W1A 4ES
Printed in Great Britain by
Western Printing Services Ltd, Bristol

ISBN 0 900821 07 8

Contents

INTRODUCTION *page* 7

LETTERS: 1909   14

LETTERS: 1910   44

EPILOGUE   75

NOTES   76

Introduction

'Oh for exercise and slumber, long fasting and full meals. Oh to forget all my scruples and live a while in peace and freedom and for the moment only, in a place where all is absent which can stimulate to moral feeling. I am sick of morals. Aren't you?' That is how Frederick Rolfe, self-styled Baron Corvo, closes a letter to Richard Dawkins, the Professor of modern Greek at Oxford who a few days later took him on holiday to Venice. With his belongings packed in a laundry basket, a massive crucifix on his chest and an enormous fountain pen filled with red ink, Rolfe left England in the late summer of 1908.

Frederick William Rolfe, the eldest son of a family of six children, was born in Cheapside, London, in 1860. His father's family had for three generations been manufacturers of musical instruments. Rolfe's education was erratic; after leaving school at fourteen he became a pupil teacher, and later a 'tosher', or unattached student at Oxford. He came down without graduating and worked as an assistant master in several provincial schools. Rolfe had from boyhood been drawn to the religious life – he was brought up as a Protestant – and his plans for a career in the church were formed in adolescence. In 1886, at twenty-five, he became a convert to Catholicism. Shortly afterwards he began studying for the priesthood, at Oscott. Here he received the tonsure, but after nine months was dismissed for unexplained reasons. A year later he resumed his training for the priesthood, at the Scots College in Rome, but the independence and perversity which were to mark and embitter his entire life soon manifested themselves, leading to unpopularity and eventually to his discharge. This painful episode was to cause him life-long frustration and deepen the shadow of his isolation and sense of persecution.

Rejected, he returned to England, adopted the pseudonym Baron Corvo and began a life which, in its richness of incident and variety of adventure, is scarcely to be matched. For eight years he travelled about – Graham Greene has called them 'the purgatorial years' – turning his hand to painting, photography, tutoring, inventing and journalism.

Tired at last of his wanderings, Rolfe came to London in 1899, now nearly forty, and began writing. His literary career starts with the publication in *The Yellow Book* of a series of short stories based on Italian folk tales. These 'Stories Toto Told Me,' caused a considerable stir but brought their author scant financial reward. A historical work,

BARON CORVO

Chronicles of the House of Borgia, followed in 1901; again it was praised by the critics but found only a limited public. His next book was a novel called *Hadrian the Seventh* (1904), in which he saw himself as Pope. D. H. Lawrence described this remarkable work as 'a clear and definite book of our epoch, not to be swept aside. If it is the book of a demon, as Corvo's contemporaries said, it is the book of a man demon, not a mere *poseur*. And if some of it is caviare, at least it came out of the belly of a live fish.' Graham Greene has written: '*Hadrian the Seventh*, a novel of genius, stands in relation to the other novels of its day, much as *The Hound of Heaven* stands in relation to the verse.' Rolfe also wrote three historical novels, *Don Tarquinio* (1905), *Don Renato* (printed in 1909, but not published until 1963) and *Hubert's Arthur* (published posthumously in 1935); a fantastic reincarnation romance, *The Weird of the Wanderer* (1912), and a semi-autobiographical novel, *Nicholas Crabbe* (1958).

The letters that follow belong to the last period of Rolfe's life when he had given up the struggle to earn a living by writing in England. When the brief holiday in Venice with Professor Dawkins was over, Rolfe refused to return home with him. He had fallen in love with the city. Sailing his boat on the lagoon for whole days and nights, rowing convalescents from the English hospital, taking photographs, working long hours at his books and writing innumerable letters, time passed quickly and he ignored his mounting hotel bill.

His friends in England implored him to return. But when he squandered the money sent for his fare home, they gave him up. He reacted by writing violent letters. No more money arrived and his landlord became threatening.

His eccentricity appealed to the Venetians and he made many friends. The story goes that one day, rounding a sharp bend in the Grand Canal too suddenly, Rolfe fell overboard while smoking his pipe. Swimming underwater he surfaced, unexpectedly far from his boat, looking serenely oblivious, with his pipe still in his mouth. On clambering into the craft he briskly knocked out the wet tobacco, refilled, borrowed a light and with the single word *Avanti!* went his way. The Venetians were delighted by the incident and elected him a member of the city's fashionable rowing club.

Hopelessly in arrears with his bill, Rolfe, was at length turned out of his hotel. From now on he was to be completely homeless for months on end, sometimes living in an open boat and often driven to tramping the streets. He subsisted for a time on only two small bread rolls a day. Once he ate nothing at all for a week. Instead of tobacco he smoked stewed tea leaves. At one point he worked as a gondolier for an alcoholic English painter and his family. 'I have been earning two meals of one plate a day by gondoliering,' he writes in a letter; 'the job keeps me alive, fairly serene though I am apparently robbed of my literary

INTRODUCTION

career as of 10 years' work. But I am not humbled, nor will be. Better by far to wear ruin as a diadem.' Soon the strain became unbearable. 'I bore it as long as I could,' he said. 'But when, after slaving for him all day, he cursed me and expected me to eat my rice two hours late in his water-closet, I left him.'

Like Rousseau, Rolfe attracted admirers and friends eager to help him. But like Rousseau, too, he was paranoid and invariably became tormented by pathological suspicion and subjected them to bitter invective. In fact most of his time and talent were now spent writing vituperative postcards and letters. He was convinced that his friends in England and fellow British residents desired his death. Actually they were merely annoyed by his antics and dismayed by his stubborn refusal to return home. Horatio Brown, a pillar of the Anglo-American colony in Venice, invited him to his Monday evening stag-parties. Though Rolfe disliked the company there, he continued to go 'in the frantic hope of finding a biscuit or a sandwich on the sideboard'. Following the inevitable quarrel, he haunted a certain canal with the express purpose of publicly cutting Brown, to his extreme indignation.

But Rolfe was capable of unexpected gallantry. When the Cardinal Patriarch of Venice was molested on the Grand Canal during anti-clerical demonstrations, Rolfe leapt to his aid, offering to escort the prelate 'anywhere in my bark under banner of England guaranteeing perfect security'. In recognition of this courtesy, the Cardinal named him his 'gondolier extraordinary'.

He was not to remain a free-lance gondolier for long, for in the late summer of 1909 he found refuge in the home of an English doctor. It was here he wrote the greater part of his Venetian romance, *The Desire and Pursuit of the Whole*, in which he lampooned certain British residents. Reading this book – 'rancid with libel' – one day the doctor's wife recognized friends of hers and demanded that Rolfe should either stop writing it or leave. He left immediately, a decision which ultimately cost him his life.

Another period of homelessness followed – this time in bitter weather. He was taken to hospital with pneumonia, bronchitis and heart trouble and given the Last Rites, but recovered. When a fund was organized by the British colony, to secure his repatriation, he used the proceeds to return, not to England, but to his former hotel, where he was given a sunless den and obliged to eat with the servants.

But his luck changed. He at last found a benefactor – an Anglican clergyman on holiday in Venice – who agreed to make him a regular allowance, and a new life began. With never a thought that this money would not last indefinitely, Rolfe spent lavishly. He took up residence in a Renaissance palace on the Grand Canal. The walls of his bedroom were hung with scarlet brocade, with curtains, bedcoverings and cushions to match. His private craft, with elaborately-painted silken sails, was manned – as for royalty – by four gondoliers. John Cowper Powys recalls in his *Autobiography* an encounter with this 'floating equipage that resembled the barge of Cleopatra, or . . . that ship, so often delineated in Greek vase paintings, that carried the great god Dionysus on his triumphant voyage'. Rolfe was reclining in the stern on a leopard skin.

One of his most spectacular escapades occurred at the funeral of Lady Layard, a respected member of the British colony. Infuriated by not being invited, Rolfe turned up outside the church dressed in the crimson robes and tasselled hat of a cardinal and, as the coffin passed, hurled insulting epithets, to the disgust of the mourners.

After a year he had spent all. To his benefactor he wrote pathetically, in a sudden change of tone: 'I am so awfully lonely. And tired. Is there no chance of setting me straight?' But the long struggle was over. Rolfe died suddenly in the autumn of 1913, aged 53.

All that is best and worst in Rolfe can be learnt from these years in Venice. He was proud, quarrelsome, perverse, over-bearing, vindictive, stubborn, ungrateful, self-centred and cadging. Nevertheless, he had his virtues. He was genuinely kind, a fascinating companion when he chose, he was industrious and he had the excuse of extreme poverty for the habit of sponging. Gifted at many points – Rolfe excelled as a swimmer, sculler, musician, photographer, painter and scribe – his best medium of self-expression he found in books and letters, although these brought him little success. Rolfe was a man obsessed and his works bear an impression of the energy with which he persisted, vainly seeking a way out of his self-imposed martyrdom.

The recipient of the Venice Letters was Charles Masson Fox. Born at Falmouth in 1866, the younger son of a merchant, he came from a staunch and highly respected Quaker family. Fox was educated at Falmouth Grammar School, Honiton, and Sherborne. After serving in various offices he joined his father's timber firm, of which he eventually became senior partner. He was also for many years on the board of an old-established shipping agency. In addition to his business interests, Fox was Russian and Swedish Vice-Consul in Falmouth for several years.

Fox was a quiet-mannered, retiring man. Of average build and height, he had a round face, large eyes under thick brows and a prominent moustache. In politics he was a Liberal and took an active part in the affairs of his home town. His principal recreation was chess, in which he distinguished himself as an amateur.

Among Fox's narrow circle of friends were J. G. F. Nicholson, schoolmaster and minor poet, Henry Tuke, the painter, both of whom are referred to in this correspondence, and Louis Marlow, the novelist and essayist, who met Rolfe several times in Venice during 1912. Marlow writes:

INTRODUCTION

I knew Masson Fox well. He was a man of unusual character. He showed his courage by bringing an action for blackmail against a woman who demanded money from him with threats that, if he did not pay, she would make it known that he had seduced her son. He was entirely innocent of this, but in those days the prosecutor for blackmail had to have his own name in the papers and could not be described as 'Mr X.' Fox won his case with no difficulty, but his bringing it was highly prejudicial to his timber business in Falmouth and in other ways too. His life was more or less uneventful, but as a person he was unique in my experience. In some ways he was the embodiment of traditional Quakerism, though he was not an adherent to the Quaker religion. 'What is it about him that's so different?' I remember my mother saying after she first met him. And then she added, 'I know! I think he must be a Quaker!' He could silence the noisy and intrusive simply by being silent. I have seen him do it: it was his presence. I had the impression that Fox got tired of Corvo's difficult nature after some while and stopped trying to help him. But he was reticent on this matter.

Fox lived most of his life at Falmouth and died unmarried there in 1935.

The circumstances of Rolfe's meeting with Fox and his 'wealthy' American friend Cockerton are not recorded, but the meeting evidently took place in Venice during the late summer of 1909. Their mutual friend John Gambril Nicholson may well have been responsible for introducing them. Acquaintance and sympathy soon ripened into friendship. With Rolfe letter-writing was almost a mania, so it is not surprising that soon after Fox's departure he struck up a correspondence with him.

It is quite clear that Rolfe was at this time obsessed with adolescent boys. It is obvious that Masson Fox was also strongly attracted to boys. 'That homosexual underworld,' of which A. J. A. Symons tells us that Rolfe 'stood self-revealed as patron', was in fact a little circle of three or four young, ragged lads ('simple little devils', Rolfe calls them) in their late 'teens, with whom he was on terms of intimate friendship. Besides these he refers in passing to half-a-dozen others. He delighted in picking their brains and listening to their tales. Symons also claims that Rolfe had become 'a habitual corrupter of youth' and 'a seducer of innocence', but the letters reveal that all three youths were practised initiates long before Rolfe set foot in Venice and so were neither innocent nor chaste. But they were genuinely fond of Rolfe and eager to meet a friend who shared their tastes.

It is significant that the twenty-year vow of celibacy, which Rolfe had taken in 1890 on his rejection from the priesthood, did not end until early in 1910, when he wrote to the Archbishop of Westminster, reminding him that:

[I am] still a Tonsured Clerk and persisting in my Divine Vocation to the priesthood. I should say also, that my vow of twenty years' celibacy (which I offered in proof of my Vocation) expires this year, and that I am not at all moved to avail myself of liberty, but propose to renew my vow for life at the year's end.

'At the year's end' – this letter was written on January 5th 1910! Three weeks later he throws off all restraint and takes young Peter to Burano, an event which he describes to Fox in explicit detail.

Obviously Rolfe never expected this correspondence to be published. Indeed in the opening letter he asks Fox to destroy his letters. Fox's side of the correspondence has perished, though he chose to save Rolfe's.

For forty years the Venice Letters have existed in a penumbra of curiosity, scandal and speculation. Much nonsense has been written and many fantastic rumours have circulated. Few documents so notorious have been so little known at first hand and their publication may serve to clear the air of some of the cant and hysteria which they have generated.

Recalling his immediate reaction on first reading the letters, A. J. A. Symons could write:

How well I remember that midnight when, alone in my tiny study, I sat down to read [them] . . . and as I read my hair began to rise. Here, described with the frank felicity of *Hadrian the Seventh*, was an unwitting account, step by step, of the destruction of a soul. The idealism of George Arthur Rose, the generous sentiments and hopes for man and the world which distinguish *Hadrian*, were not to be found in these pages. On the contrary, they gave an account, in language that omitted nothing, of the criminal delights that waited for the ignoble sensualist to whom they were addressed. . . . Only lack of money, it appeared, prevented the writer from enjoying an existence compared with which Nero's was innocent, praiseworthy, and unexciting: indeed, it seemed that even without money he had successfully descended to depths from which he could hardly hope to rise. Throughout all the letters one purpose was visible: they were an entreaty to their recipient to bring his wealth to a market where it would buy full value. Rolfe could answer for the wares he offered: he had tested them, and he would willingly be guide to this earthly paradise. . . . What shocked me about these letters was not the confession they made of perverse sexual indulgence: that phenomenon surprises no historian. But that a man of education, ideas, something near genius, should have enjoyed without remorse the destruction of the innocence of youth; that he should have been willing for a price to traffic in his knowledge of the dark byways of that Italian city; that he could have pursued the paths of lust with such frenzied tenacity: these things shocked me into anger and pity.

INTRODUCTION

A. E. Housman observed, in writing to Grant Richards, the publisher, that he had 'been more amused with things written in urinals'. Symons also called them 'letters that Aretino might have written at Casanova's dictation'.

A more balanced reaction, however, is that of Pamela Hansford Johnson, who has written:

> I do not think the Venice Letters can be written off as easily as some would like – neither for good nor ill. For there really is something splendid, almost mythological, about their ramping sexuality; it was so extremely wholehearted, as everything about him was. If one must read this kind of thing, Rolfe is incomparably better at it than Henry Miller. And there are a few passages of descriptive splendour as fine as anything in *The Desire and Pursuit of the Whole*, where the physical beauty of Venice is expressed as no one else ever did it, before Rolfe or after him.

But the letters are not only an addition to sensual literature. For as *The Desire and Pursuit of the Whole* indicates, Rolfe is looking for something more satisfying than physical sensuality alone. The main themes of that novel are loneliness and above all the search for the 'other half', in the Platonic context of the title, a search for union. The Venice Letters show that like many people of all sorts of sexual concerns, Rolfe wanted a body, without personal commitment, and yet also a person, a human being. In short he wanted to love and be loved only when he chose. The distaste he expresses for younger boys, because he couldn't see their faces when he was having sex with them, is significant. 'Where are the sparkling eyes, in whose depths I may see the ripple of pleasure?' Rolfe clearly feels that personal commitment is necessary, but his problem is how to make it. One of the principal themes of *Hadrian the Seventh* is the hero's inability to love. In the famous prayer early in the novel he says:

> You well know that You have made me all-denuded of the power of loving anybody, of the power of being loved by any. Self-contained, You have made me. I shall always be detached and apart from others.

It is this concern for involvement that adds depth to the Venice Letters.

C.W.

1909

I[1]

[No place or date]

Tuesday: but I shall have to wait for your address before I can post this.

Before I forget it, I have not received any particulars of E.[2] from Cockerton;[3] and I should very much like to have the Florentine addresses *in order of merit*.

I have never seen anything so comical as what happened after you left. I gave you the main facts, and now I will add particulars: but first I must tell you that, about five minutes after I had posted my last card to you, the Corfiote Greek Jew actually came here to see me (a thing he had never done before, our acquaintance being merely a club[4] one), with a full and urgent offer of service. Fausto had told him what was wanted, and it appears that he is very anxious to employ himself in such a capacity, having heard about it, liking the idea, and (– This is simply damnable. I have this moment been interrupted by a telephone call from my typhoidic friend[5] – a thing HE has never done before – asking me to meet him tonight and saying that his brother Saverio, a lion-cub of 13, wants to go out in my sandolo! The tortures of Tantalus were nothing to this.) – being dreadfully frightened of the method usual among his companions. He was delightfully delicate about it; and his English (I have told you that he knows English) was well worth writing down. I thanked him very much, told him that my friends were gone to England on business for the present, and regretted that as far as I personally was concerned, my poverty prevented me from taking any steps in the matter, at least for the present. He was a little offended; and I had rather a bother to make him understand that no offence was intended but that I simply meant that I was tied to this house and had no place in which to entertain him at present. But I think you'll agree that a non-mercenary Greek Jew of Corfu is worth cultivating when possible if only for his rarity. However, to go back to P. & G. and to C. and little G.[6] Knowing that their weak spot is their vanity,

VENICE LETTERS

I didn't beat about the bush but just took them separately, and put them in a good humour by buying them a white linen suit and jersey each with a red sash. I am alluding to P. and G. his brother and C. And to each one I described what was wanted in the way of service. Of course they said, that was what they expected. So I suppose they understood the indications which you and Cockerton must have given though I'm bound to say that I was quite unaware of anything definite. And they were not only willing but glad to do whatever was required. I said that they would be wanted two at a time, and that I would send them orders when I got your instructions. I did this because it was useless to take P. to Burano on Monday,[7] he having expressed his willingness without persuasion – and impossible because I had drained myself on the clothes. Then, Saturday night, comes P. here, very modest and diffident, ostensibly to 'salute' me. After a lot of charming rambling, his real object oozed out or was squeezed out of him. His friend G. (not his little brother G. mind you) was so desolate in spirit at being out of it, regretted his foolish behaviour of last year, wanted me to forgive him and regard him favourably in future, had practised regularly with P. since March and would I kindly let him have another chance of displaying his skill and accomplishments. I said yes with pleasure, took him out and bought him a uniform like the others and told him that I would give him and P. an engagement when in a position to do so. So I was all ready for your definite statement of arrival; and should have given you and Cockerton the pick of the bunch. Frankly, you know, I couldn't undertake anything on my own account till I had fulfilled my obligations. Of course one can't admire the slavish tendency. But I firmly maintain that the best method is to begin with slaves and educate them out of slavery into intelligent and faithful servants. Well: then came Cockerton's telephone and your telegram and subsequent letter. I lay low through them all, until it was quite certain that you were not coming back. Then I paid myself out of the L. 20[8] (for which thanks) the extra L. 11.50 which I had spent on their clothes and went round telling them that you had been suddenly called to England and dividing the balance of L. 9.50 between them to console them for their disappointment. They were grieved but sweet about it, excepting little G. whom I don't like any more than does his brother P. That was the best which I could conceive: for I didn't want there to be any doubts this time, and it's always safer with Venetians to arrange so that you can have your pick; because one or other is nearly certain to fail at the crucial moment.

I'm frightfully sorry you couldn't come back to enjoy the fun: but I'm not at all sorry to have had the experience, because now I know that when the gods are good enough to let me have a week to myself at Burano I can always get P. and G. to share it with me. If only I had a little place of my own, though, think of the visits of the Greek, and the typhoid, and his brother Saverio. Lord, when I think of it! Now I'm going to write like blazes.[9] Do write to me often, and freely. I'll always answer and burn your letters. Do this with mine please.

Kind regards to Cockerton. Whisper – I detest Jackson.[10]   R.

2

Palazzo Mocenigo Corner, Venice.   October 25, 1909.

Dear F.,

I am awfully glad to have your letter: I was beginning to be seriously afraid that you were not going to write. Before I go any further I want to ask you to do something for me. The state of my wardrobe is appalling and I don't know how I am going to get through the winter, keeping warm and presenting a decent appearance. It is the washing of white things which is the special difficulty. So I think that a couple of dark blue woollen jerseys would be a boon. They must be *soft*, have *high collars*, and be knitted in *perpendicular lines*. Can you without inconvenience put your hand on such a couple and send them by parcel post. If so, mark them plainly outside in English and Italian as follows:

SAMPLES. CAMPIONI SENZA VALORE.

and then I shan't have to pay duty on them, which I can't afford. Boots will have to take care of themselves and come from elsewhere.

You can't think how pleased I am that you should have noticed (and remembered) the 'manner' of P. and C. in telling their stories. Of course I notice all that kind of detail; because I am an artist. But I very rarely find another man equally observant and appreciative of these smaller and more exquisite touches which really have so pretty and satisfying a savour. All the same, though, what you saw is a very little thing compared with what you might have seen had I been free from frightful worries and had you had a little more time to spare. These Venetians, like all Orientals (for they really are Orientals you know) are frightfully shy of strangers; and it always takes time to get them to unstiffen and to let themselves go. When they do, they do it thoroughly. And that is just what happened. I do really think that all my actions and exertions of the past year only came into sudden flower at the moment when you were on the verge of going away. P. and C. and the rest knew me thoroughly by then. They had seen me in wealth and in poverty. They had got over their fear of me and knew me for one of themselves. And they also had thoroughly realized what I wanted and the benefits and personal pleasure accruing from letting me have what I wanted. Two things only – (as my manner is, I am analyzing the affair scientifically, on such evidence as I have) – prevented them from combining with me. The one thing was my pecuniary inability to do my part, viz. to provide opportunity and to make it worth their while. The other was a certain subconscious hesitation about doing the unusual, the uncustomary. For the Venetians are the slaves of 'Custom.' They fear 'Scorn' – (which only means the Charge of being Singular) more than anything else in Nature. But then you and Cock appeared; and there was no doubt but that you were of the same tastes and habits and dispositions as myself. It was evident then, to P. and C. and to the rest, that I was not singular, for there were at least two other *signori* like me. 'Well then' they argued 'we shall not be doing anything unusual, and we need not be afraid of "Scorn".' Dear simple creatures! And then, also, new clothes and money were given: and there was an opportunity of spending a day or two at Burano. So, as I imagine, they instantly threw all scruples over the windmill and were eager and ready and simply blazing to oblige us and themselves. Personally I think that Gildo's complete change of front, his fervent anxiety to go and do where Peter went and did, his simply complete ascent from sulky dignity to sparklingly brazen incontinence, was the most comical and also the most genuine and loveable feature of the whole affair. And I'm sure you can imagine far better than I can tell you the most tantalizing tortures which I suffer in consequence. To have offered the very thing that I have been yearning and still burn for, offered unreservedly, and not to be able even to touch it. Peter I know would gladly enter into my service and be a good zealous and obedient servant, at any moment when I was able to take him. And I ask nothing better. *But to have to refuse him for a whole year, and now to have to refuse Gildo too* – oh, it is too bitter. Do you see and sympathize with my position? I hope you do. And, of course, if you can think of any way of getting me out of my pickle and on my feet again, for Heaven's sake let me know. In return, beside the usual return, I'll engage to have your place and servants ready for you here at any time and for as long as you like. I am a powerful person and I loathe and detest to grind with all my might against this damnable impotence which chains me at present. The worst of it is I am so worn out that I have nothing at present to suggest. I seem to be at the end of my ideas, for the solution of my difficulties and I really don't believe I shall be able to think out plans, other than those already proposed, until I've had at least a week's rest and change of occupation either at Florence or with P. or G. in my service at Burano. *I'm simply bunged-up.* Moreover, I must tell you that I've had another smack in the face since I saw you. I think I told you that a new literary agent in London had been recommended to me and that I had sent him £180 sterling's worth of Venetian essays and stories. Well: now he has suddenly seen fit to fail;[11] and, instead of having that £180 stg to go on with (which would clear off a few of my embarrassments and give me some sort of a chance), here I have all that stuff returned and lying fallow on my hands again just because I can't exploit it properly myself. Beside that, I'm very much afraid that my host here is in a bad way. It's not joyful, living with a pious crank, eating cranky food sauced with the most unctuous of rancid piety. But I'm practically certain that even that is going to be snatched away from me.[12] He has no patients and says he is living on God. How would you feel, if you were me, when a married man with a family talks like that, saying that he can't pay either his rent or his insurance? All I know is that it makes me so sick that I can't digest his food. Oh, Lord! So you see, I live in the midst of alarms. And you won't, I know, expect anything particularly cheerful from me. N.B. Anyhow let me have the other addresses. *I have not had Eduardo's yet.* Remember that I will look out for places here, as often as I can shew myself decently in public. At present I can't. And today is the first rain and cold and how one is going to get through the winter, Evan only knows.

WRITE OFTEN.   R.

VENICE LETTERS

3

Pal. Moc. Cor.

[No date]

Dear F.,

Every day I live here something hurts me. No – this is something different to what I generally say. I have just touched upon it to you in conversation: but, the longer I live the more convinced I am that I shan't be happy until I have set it down in a written form, which you can shew to those whom it concerns. It may jog them: or it may not. Anyhow, I shall have relieved my mind of a burthen.

(*a*) One thing which this world wants is some Tuke[13] pictures of the Venetian lagoon and some Tuke pictures of mediaeval *gondoglieri* poised on *poppe* in Venetian canals.

(*b*) But 'Tuke has all he wants at Falmouth.' Hum! Arnold of Rugby held that no man ought to be a school-master longer than 15 years at a stretch. And I fancy that the principle of that doctrine may apply to painters. By stagnating in one place and on one subject or kind of subject, they prevent themselves from much delight and the world from much glory. Tuke has made himself an immortal name with the flesh and sun and sea of Falmouth. He cannot possibly better it; and by persistence he may very likely worsen it. I (being an artist[14]) know quite well that he hasn't satisfied himself. But an artist never does. The thing is for him to know that he has worked in one groove long enough; and, for his own and his art's sake to try another.

(*c*) I suggest to him Venice. No Englishman paints Venice excepting the kaleidoscopic Brangwyn[15] and a mob of little lookers-through-smoked-glasses who paint in dirty earths and soap and wax. I am not talking of the Montalbas.[16] And the only Venetian (Italian) worth talking about who paints it is Giuseppe Miti-Zanetti,[17] who uses a process of his own, neither oil nor water, which certainly is wonderful, but purely architectural and atmospheric and generally nocturnal. Which signifies that a painter like Tuke would have a free field here: for there is not a single painter of young Venetians, poised, ('poise' is the unique characteristic) poised on lofty poops, out on the wide wide lagoon, at white dawn, when the whole world gleams with the candid iridescence of mother of pearl, glowing white flesh with green-blue eyes and shining hair poised in white air trembling like song in white light reflected in white smooth sea – of young Venetians poised on lofty poops out on the wide lagoon, at high noon, when all the world which is not brilliant is blue, glowing young litheness with its sumptuous breast poised in air like showers of acquamarines on a sapphire sea with shadows of lapis-lazuli under a monstrous dome of turquoise – of young Venetians poised on lofty poops out on the wide lagoon, at sunset, glowing magnificent young strength dominantly illumined, poised in an atmosphere of lavender and heliotrope in tremendous stretches of sea and sky all cut out of jewels, limitless amethyst and far-reaching turquoise, or, all burnished copper splashed with emeralds and streaked with blue, the insistent blue of borage. No one does these things: no one sees them, but me. But Tuke is the only man alive who can do them; and he has not seen them. And who but Tuke could do *real* mediaeval *gondoglieri* in long fantastically striped hosen of silk, proud in the pomp of brocade, poised on lofty poops in the luminous shade of some small canal by some wonderful old water-gate like the Casa Agnusdei, or that of the Casa Amore degli Amici, or the one of the Calle Tedeum? No one. And he does not. It is dismal.

(*d*) But he wants to race with the yachts. Maria Vergine, isn't there a whole line of racing yachts anchored off the Bucintoro terrace? Isn't the only thing necessary an accomplished English yachtsman to come and simply rule this roost?

(*e*) In short can't he have here *better*, and *different*, flesh, shapes, sun, sea, light, shade, opportunities, pleasures, than he can have at Falmouth? Then why rust there? I guarantee not to speak to him. And now I have done my best to free my mind.   R.

4

Pal. Moc. Cor.   November 8, [1909].

Dear F.,

I wrote enclosed last week; and kept it to send off if you should answer me. It is just a scrap of conversation – an idea which I should have spoken in words if you had been here. Just take it for what it is, please. I am awfully obliged to you for the guernsey. If I could have them like that, but with perpendicular lines and a little longer in the sleeves and higher in the collar, I should be delighted. Please see how much they are: for there is a chance that, if I can scratch up enough to get through this month and conduct certain negotiations which I will tell you about in a minute, all my difficulties will be solved and I shall be in full funds. By the bye, when you send them, for Evan's sake send your letter separately. I had to pay L. 2.65 for this parcel which means no tobacco after Friday.

This is what has happened. You remember that Scheme which was sent to Skeels?[18] It has been taken up by a firm of solicitors in London who have (I'm told) the reputation of doing unusual business. They say that there needn't be any difficulty. They can find me a financial partner and undertake the proper management of my assets. The question now with me is how to make Barnard and Taylor[19] let go. I suppose B. & T. only want money. You see it's absolutely impossible for them to get a farthing without my assent, which I flatly refuse to give under present circumstances. Consequently I have hung up my books.[20] They want them published. I won't have them published till I'm secure of getting some at least of the profits. So I have written to B. & T. severely, but politely, telling [them] that I am prepared to transfer my property, or rather to redeem it from them. Meanwhile though, as you'll well understand, it's necessary to make a good impression on these new people. I've always found that no one will have anything to do with a person who seems to need it, though *everyone is anxious to deal with a person who appears to want to have nothing to do with them.* So the last is the line I am taking and if I'm hung up for stamps or things I shall say 'damn' loud. If this thing comes off and I get clear and some money in my pocket to play with I shall take a month's holiday and bring Peter and Carlo to England and live at an hotel at Falmouth where I can return your hospitality in a way which would enchant you. I have only seen them once since my last: but they are keener than ever. It was fearfully funny. I have been sticking entirely indoors, for reasons, and simply writing myself blind over this new book. But last Monday and Tuesday were great days here. All Saints and All Souls.[21] So I went across the lagoon on the bridge of boats to the cemetery at Sanmichele. All Venice was there with candles and flowers and lamps, decorating the graves of their dead.

You never saw such gorgeousness of a garden. And the crowd! Well: I was slowly sauntering along a path, rather grim and sad myself being lonely and all that, when I spied Peter and Carlo and Gildo and Giuseppe and four more (one quite lovely and quite unknown to me, but smallish), quietly and silently kneeling on their wicked knees round the grave of one of their comrades and praying for the repose of his soul. They had clubbed together and got 6 lire of candles and 4 of flowers; and they had grubbed up the past year's weeds with their abominable hands and made the thing neat and pretty, simply for love, quite frankly and utterly without shame. I spotted them in the tail of my eye, passed, and did not interrupt, chiefly because I was poor as well as abashed. But one of them spotted me. I heard someone say *'Ecco'l paron!'* ('There's the Master!') And the next minute they were all over me with their cheerful friendly salutations. It was charming. Never have I seen anything like the eyes of Gildo or a skin as white. Carlo was keen to enquire after *"l Sior Volpe'* (meaning you, for I told them that was your name, they being quite unable to get nearer Fox than *Focassa* with their Venetian tongues). So then I went back to the grave and they shewed me their work with naïve pride, which of course I praised. And we walked about to admire the other graves for quite an hour, sometimes one with me, sometimes another, and all of them taking occasion to say to me privately 'Sior when shall we go to Burano for the night?' Oh Lord! But, ISN'T IT COMICAL? If you only had come to me directly you arrived in Venice? Or if only I hadn't been fettered as I am!

Have you got the other Florentine addresses yet? Or Eduardo's? The latter seems to be rather a Mrs Harris.[22] This is a dull letter. But I can't get out and about. The pupparin is quite useless, leaks like a sieve, ought to have gone to the *squero* to be mended months ago. I haven't paid my subscription to the 'Bucintoro' and don't like to shew my face there. So I have to stick on this landing where I live, and write as best I can. It's a treat (and my only one) to have someone to talk to like this. Keep in close touch with me please.

                     Yrs, R.

VENICE LETTERS

5

Thursday [Probably toward the end of November 1909].

Dear C.,

Thanks for yours of 20th. Addresses duly noted: but can't find Via Niccolini on map. What is it near? I'll give photos to P. and C. when I see them, two to each. I'll keep the boat one if you don't mind in memory of such a decent day. As to what C. was thinking about, I suppose it was it. It always was huge; and, since he left my service in the spring, he has begun that period of life which makes it a more prominent feature in one's economy. Now this is very funny indeed – (By the bye, please on no account shew my letters to Nicholson[23] or give him any of my news. He is *dangerous*.) – *It appears that I know Eduardo Bolck well*; and have known him for a year, without the slightest suspicion of his amusements. He belongs to the 'Bucintoro'; and used to be there continually in spring and early summer, when I (having no home at all) spent most of my days drowsing there *so that I should be fit to prowl about in the pupparin all night.* E., I admired immensely and would have given anything to make his acquaintance. But we never got beyond *'Buongiorno'* and a change of smiles of which I now and only now know the meaning. I can see now quite well that he was hanging about to give me a chance. I'll tell you why I say that. I always used to think it funny that he sat reading and rereading the papers in whichever room I was; and wondered what in the world his avocation was. And, one day, I found out that he was perfectly aware of everything I did or said there. There was the usual row with Fausto for not cleaning my boat. I made a long speech of abuse in Italian. And it's a Venetian dodge when found out by an English to pretend that he's unintelligible. So Fausto gaped and said *'Mi no go capio'* 'I don't understand' in Venetian. Instantly, before I could call him a pigeon-eating son of a priest, and translate my Italian into Venetian, Bolck (without looking up from his paper) cannonaded down Fausto's throat 'You know very well what this lord has said. He said so and so, you potato, you marionette, fox and vile one.' Which of course means that, though he was sitting at the other end of the room, he was taking a friendly and extremely intimate interest in my affairs

BARON CORVO

... Imagine then how anxious I am to go further with him ...

Well, just before you came, he got into trouble at the Club, was one of five who broke a boat, and got posted to pay his share of damages. This I saw. Three paid, the 2 Bolcks never. (I don't know the brother.) *And Eduardo ceased coming to the Club.* I suppose that's why he frequented the Lido. So, last week, I sent a card (closed) to the address you gave me, saying that I should like to meet him to deliver a message from his *American* friend at the Grand. But I have had no answer and don't know how to find him. He may be away; he may be frightened (though that's unlikely) or the address may be insufficient. That is most likely: for you did not give me *the number of the house* and 'Via 22 Marzo' only means 'Twenty-second of March Street,' the twenty-second of March being the anniversary of some Venetian victory over the Austrians. If I could find him I should say that his friend and mine salutes him and wishes to know that he has got a job, and if he likes to write I'll translate his letter into *American* and forward it. Of course I may butt into him in the streets. If I do I shall say the same. *But it's out of my power to do more, yet awhile.* This is why. The negotiations which I spoke of in my last have broken down, and I am back on my beam ends to begin all over again. I had got a firm of solicitors to consider the question of taking over my obligations and assets. They were satisfied with what I could shew them and named a day for seeing the things which my present agents and Pirie-Gordon[24] have of mine. I wrote P-G and my agents asking them to consent to shew what they have. And they didn't answer till after the day. Consequently the other people took fright and said it was off very naturally. Of course it's extremely damnable. I don't for a moment expect any luck till I am able to move for myself. There the things are and absolutely useless to anyone (as my present agents confess with curses) unless I take off the embargo I have laid on them. And, as I told you, I flatly refuse to do that until I have them in my own hands, or in the hands of some one who'll manage them properly. They shall not be mismanaged any longer. And it's impossible for me to get them till I have a place to put them in, the cost of their transit, and say three clear months to work them. *For that I want a sum.* I've got £80 worth of stories running round the magazines just now, secretly, and no one has any lien at all on them; and I have three-parts finished my new book called *The Desire and Pursuit of the Whole which I also am free to assign.* And meanwhile I can't tell you how utterly beastly miserable it makes me to take the P.O.O. which you kindly sent me. I suppose it was for me? I hope to goodness it was; for I don't know how I could go on without it. The fact is this last fortnight has been absolutely Devilish. No tobacco, Alps covered with snow, *bora* blowing up Adriatic one day and wind from Alps bringing simply perishing cold. And here I live and work and sleep on an *open landing* of this palace on the side which never sees the sun with *stone* floor, walls, ceiling and stairs, no privacy (it's the servants' stair) and *no heating arrangements whatever.* I haven't even seen a fire. And I have but one thin blanket. My dear, *I'm simply dying of cold and hunger.* The doctor is a dear. If he didn't give me this hospitality I should be on the streets and that would be the end of all my hopes. But you see, it would be ungracious to ask for more. Besides, if I did, he would be shocked, and I shouldn't get anything. He thinks that hardships ought to be welcomed because they teach us patience and make us hardy. So they do; and he's right in a way. BUT – this is fact, I have got a certain long difficult job to do requiring knowledge, perseverance, concentration, and *incessant toil at full speed.* All these qualities I have, and the will as well as the most earnest desire to use them. *But I am only able to do less than half what I could do, because I'm (as I said) perished with cold and hunger.* I want proper clothes, warmth, light, and beef and wine. (Thanks to you I've had a gorge of the last two on the sly today and now I'm smoking!) And I want all sorts of other things which God knows how I'm going to get. But anyhow, till I get a Sum, something decent, to work with, I shall have to put up with my present miseries. I wish I'd known you years ago. You see, *I can walk about and keep warm enough and amuse myself fairly, as I am. But, if I loaf, I can't do my work. And I want to do my work. I must do it* . . . Yes, do send me the confession. I want to see it particularly. I'll tell you why; and that will enable me also to explain my meaning about Nicholson. You must know that I know by heart all the books (ancient and modern) on the subject; and I always maintain that the modern ones are vulgar, cloying, inartistic, because they are written by amateurs. And I have also said that I could write two books (certainly two) which would have *a rattling good story* in them, *told artistically with a vividness and a plain-spokenness hitherto unheard of.* Such books, privately published in Paris or Antwerp at £1 would sell like blazes. Well, talking like this to Nich, I wrote a specimen 10,000 words or so, giving it as my personal experiences; and sent the MS. to him for discussion. I thought that he and Victor[25] would be able to give some unique criticisms in the shape of *their* personal experiences, which we all know must be singularly pretty – Victor now being of an age and education to provide an intelligent analysis of his side of the question. Well: the result was startling. I'll give it in the order it occurred. (1) Nich wrote voluminously, shrieks of joy, and descriptions of his own experiences (written however in a style precisely like that of the storiettes pencilled up in the jakes at the Marble Arch) vulgar and commonplace beyond words, and shewing a total absence of the faculties of observing detail, of perceiving fine shades of difference, and so on, without which a man cannot possibly write a pleasurably-readable description of anything, much less of what is and can be the most idyllic thing in this world. (Incidentally it came out that he was a Born Pathic.) (2) Victor got up on his hind legs and preached at me. (3) Nicholson ditto. (4) Both implored me not to write any more of what I had written. (5) N. said he couldn't keep my writing and even *was going to expunge it from his mind* because it made him feel more wicked than he had believed it possible for anyone to be –, and, at the same time, the thing was so beautiful that he didn't dare to destroy it. (Oh yes; and he felt it his duty to renounce the embraces of Victor.) (6) Naturally I sat still, roaring with laughter at such a precious and pestilent pair of prigs. (7) Ten weeks later, I took the liberty of asking the meaning of his complete and sudden change of front after his previous hysterical ecstasies of joy. (8) He evaded an answer. (9) I said 'WHAT ARE YOU AFRAID OF?' (10) 'Of being false to my ideal' he whimpered. (11) Laughing louder than ever, I asked what had happened to my literary work, which he couldn't keep even in his mind, and daren't destroy, and yet hadn't the decency to return to me. (12) He had told Edward Carpenter[26] about it – and – then – burned it! ! ! Well: so I say, in the absence of further explanations, a man who could behave with such duplicity and cant, and who could take such a damned liberty with a writer's MSS, is not only a hypocrite but a dangerous person. The unscrupulous way in which he stole my sonnet and printed it in his book years ago, was bad enough.[27] I thought he had grown out of that dirty habit. But this theft of my MS. beats all. Comments please.

To-day I have had adventures. This morning I bought a pair of boots and a kilogramme of tobacco. Lunched here, stewed celery, dry toast, water. Afterwards went to the Bonvecchiati, had a steak and a litre of red wine (the new vintage which is just in and very heady); and then, feeling up to any devilry, went smoking for a long walk through Cannareggio into the Ghetto to look for Jews. For mind you, a satisfactory Jew is worth a dozen Gentiles. They have more spunk about them somehow. I saw one whom I am going to watch as likely to be ready next spring. From there I got over to the station bridge and by a long round to the harbour end of Zattere. A Sicilian ship was lying alongside the quay and armies of lusty youths were dancing down long long planks with sacks on their shoulders which they delivered in a warehouse ashore. The air was filled with a cloud of fine white floury dust from the sacks which powdered the complexions of their carriers most deliciously and the fragrance of it was simply heavenly. As I stopped to look a minute one of the carriers attracted my notice. They were all half naked and sweating. I looked a second time as his face seemed familiar. He was running up a plank. And he also turned to look at me. Seeing my gaze he made me a sign for a cigarette. I grabbed at my pockets but hadn't got one; and shook my head. He ran on into the ship. I ran off to the nearest baccy shop and came back with a packet of cigs and a box of matches to wait at the foot of his plank. Presently he came down the plank dancing staggering under a sack. I watched him. Such a lovely figure, young, muscular, splendidly strong, big black eyes, rosy face, round black head, scented like an angel. As he came out again running (they are watched by guards all the time) I threw him my little offering. 'Who are you?' '*Amadeo Amadei*' (lovely mediaeval name). The next time, 'What are you carrying?' '*Lily-flowers for soap-making.*' The next time, 'Where have I seen you?' '*Assistant gondolier one day with Piero last year*' – then – '*Sir, Round Table –*' My dear F. I'm going to that ship again to-morrow morning. I want to know more. I couldn't stay longer to-day because of the guards but I shall try to get Amadeo Amadei to some *trattoria* for his lunch. I have a faint remembrance of his face, but only a faint one. It's as though he had grown up suddenly. I expect he was some raggamuffin whom Peter scratched up once suddenly, and since then he has developed wonderfully. And of course, Peter has been talking. Well, all I can say is that if this is a real Knight of the Round Table and knows his way to Caerleon, you may depend on me to collect information, which I of course will verify *the first moment I am able*. Peter, Gildo, Carlo and the Greek (and I take it also Eduardo) are private practitioners: for none of them have let slip the password. But this florescent creature one would think is a professional. However there will be news tomorrow. Here I stop to leave a blank space to show through the envelope. N.B. *'Signore'* not *'Seniore'* which means 'Elder.' Do write. I have only you to speak to.   R.

6

November 28, 1909.
Continued from Last Issue.

I had another smack in the face the next day. In the afternoon I went round to the Monte di Pietà (the government pawn-shop) being in funds, intending to pay up interest on and re-pawn two bundles of silver curiosities (antique rings, seals, chains and a massive cross) which I had put in six months ago. They were for 34 and 57 francs respectively. And I was informed that they had been sold (according to rule) that very day at 11 a.m. to a little jeweller who deals in antiquities for 7.50 more than the loan made and interest on it. Which 7.50 francs they handed over to me. I got the address of the jeweller and went to see him. After about an hour's quarrelling he let me pawn them privately with him at double rates, as I hadn't enough to redeem them: that is to say he holds them for three months more, not making me any loan but accepting double interest, 12% instead of 6%, and if I pay that I can have the things in three months at 50 and 73 francs respectively. I was frightfully upset: but what could I do?

From there I went off to the Quay of San Basegio on the Zattere to see the Knight of the Round Table. It was getting dusk and I was just in time to see his lissome muscular figure come dancing down the long plank from the ship with his last sack of dried lily flowers silhouetted against the sunset. As he passed, I said, 'Do me the pleasure to come and drink a little beaker of wine.' 'With the

VENICE LETTERS

greatest possible respect to your valorous face,' he answered, passing on. When he had delivered his load in the warehouse, he came out and joined me. While he was working he had on a pair of thin flannel trousers tightly tucked into his socks, canvas slippers, and a thin sleeveless shirt open from neck to navel. Over this, his day's work done, he wore a voluminous cloak of some thick dark stuff and a broad-brimmed hat. He flung one end of the cloak over his shoulder like a toga. I describe his attire thus particularly, for reasons which will appear later on. 'Take me,' I said, 'to a quiet wine shop where we can have much private conversation.' We went through a few back alleys to a little quay in a blind canal off the Rio Malcontent where there was a very decent wineshop kept by an apparent somnambulist. I called for a litre of New Red (very fresh and heady) at 6d. We sat at the back of the shop among the barrels, our two chairs being together on one side of the only table there. The counter with its sleepy proprietor was between us and the door; and no one else was present.

I asked him to tell me about the Round Table; and took care that he drank two glasses to my one. Of course I fed him with cigarettes. He said there was formerly a house on the Fondamenta Osmarin: but, owing to the fear which struck all Italy last year, when Austria seized Herzegovina and suddenly placed 80,000 men on the frontier where Italy has only 6,000 (remember this frontier is not 30 miles away, and Venice I know was frightened out of her wits) then the Venetians took a hatred of all Germans and went and smashed the windows, calling the boys and men there 'Eulenbergs'. Wherefore the committee (*comitato*) of the club, for it was a private club of Signiori of the very gravest respectability, moved the club to a house which they purchased at Padova, about an hour and a half by steamer and train. He said that the club used to be open day and night; and ten boys were there always ready for use. The fee was 7 fr. payment for the room and what you pleased to the boy, but you had to pay the latter in the presence of the steward and never more than 5 fr. even though you stayed all day or all night, i.e. 5 fr. and 7 fr. for 12 hours. Beside the staff, any boy could bring a Signiore. And many did, chiefly school-boys at some of the public or technical schools who liked to make a little pocket-money. But now, unfortunately, these and other Venetian boys were out of employment; for at Padova there is a great University with about

BARON CORVO

1,300 students of all ages, besides many schools; and students were generally in want of money. However, some of the Venetian unemployed occasionally have the luck to find an employer; in which case they make a little journey to Padova together, generally from Saturday to Monday, and derive mutual satisfaction from a Sabbath's concubinage. (I'm translating his Italian almost literally, because it's so comically naive.) He himself began at 13 or thereabouts in this way. One of his cousins being left an orphan suddenly came to live in his house and sleep in his bed. The cousin was 14 and, the bed being narrow, there was a certain mixture which pleased both. And suddenly both spat together. (You'd have shrieked to see his great black eyes and his big white teeth and his rosy young lily-fragrant face simply burst out laughing.) This being very diverting they hugged and hugged, belly to belly and did it again. So for many nights. Then a whore ate 80 francs of his elder brother, aet. 20, and gave him a disease, very disgraceful and perturbing to the family. Whereat, he and his cousin congratulated themselves on knowing a safer pleasure, and vowed to touch no whores. In a little while his cousin (they were both occasional gondoliers as I had suspected) heard of the Osmarin. A patron took him there. Amadeo Amadei, rather bucked, also went and asked for a job. They said 'Bring a Signore'. So he went and prayed to the Black Madonna of Spain at San Francesco della Vigna and she sent him a Count. Then he began. Many Counts and Princes and illustrious Signiori had he served there, having much strength and ingenuity in finding out ways to give pleasure, all of which pleased him too, as well as filling his pocket.

He found his patrons in this way. His first, the Count, had spoken to him on the Giardinetto where he was by chance lounging one morning, being out of work, and his shirt being open as usual, because he was appassionated for the air, the Count had stroked his breast while saying that he was a fine boy. To whom he said that he was as God made him and preferred to be naked. Upon which the Count took him to the Osmarin for the day. Thereafter, he always went with his breast bare, even in Piazza, and soon Signiori walked after him, to whom he nodded in the first discreet corner and so he gained patrons. But, since the Club was moved to Padova, it was difficult for an honest lad – he is $16\frac{1}{2}$ – to find a way of employing his nights. During the day he works as a stevedore along the Zattere

VENICE LETTERS

or in the harbour of Marittima, earning 3.50 generally, of which he has to give 3 fr. to his father, also a stevedore and earning the same. His elder brother is doing military service. His cousin gondoles for a merchant, i.e. a grocer with whom he lives and sleeps. One younger brother of 12 earns 1.50 as a milk-boy. Beside these three there are a mother and grandmother, five sisters and three small brothers to be kept out of the joint earnings of 8 fr. a day. Naturally he wants to earn money for himself.

He assured me that he knew incredible tricks for amusing his patrons. 'First, Sior, see my person,' he said. And the vivacious creature did all which follows in about 30 seconds of time. Not more. I have said that we were sitting side by side of the little table. Moving, every inch of him, as swiftly and smoothly as a cat, he stood up, casting a quick glance into the shop to make sure that no one noticed. Only the sleepy proprietor slept there. He rolled his coat into a pillow and put it on my end of the table, ripped open his trousers, stripped them down to his feet, and sat bare bottomed on the other end. He turned his shirt up right over his head, holding it in one hand, opened his arms wide and lay back along the little table with his shoulders on the pillow (so that his breast and belly and thighs formed one slightly slanting lane unbroken by the arch of the ribs, as is the case with flat distention) and his beautiful throat and his rosy laughing face strained backward while his widely open arms were an invitation. He was just one brilliant rosy series of muscles, smooth as satin, breasts and belly and groin and closely folded thighs with (in the midst of the black blossom of exuberant robustitude) a yard like a rose-tipped lance. And – the fragrance of his healthy youth and of the lily flower's dust was intoxicating. He crossed his ankles, ground his thighs together with a gently rippling motion, writhed his groin and hips once or twice and stiffened into the most inviting mass of fresh meat conceivable, laughing in my face as he made his offering of lively flesh. And the next instant he was up, his trousers buttoned, his shirt tucked in and his cloak folded around him. The litre of wine was gone. I called for another. 'Sior' he said, 'half a litre this time, with permission.' So we made it half. Would I not like to take him to Padova from Saturday till Monday? Indeed I would. Nothing better. But because I see that you, my Amadeo, (i.e. Love God, quite a Puritan name) are a most discreet youth as well as a very capable one, I shall tell you my secret: for, in fact, you shall know that I am no longer a rich English but a poor, having been ruined by certain traitors and obliged to deny myself luxuries. To hear that gave him affliction and much dolour. But he wished to say that he was all and entirely at my disposal simply for affection; because, feeling sure that he had the ability to provide me with an infinity of diversions, each different and far more exciting than its predecessor, he asked me as a favour, as a very great favour, that I should afterwards recommend him to nobles who were my friends. And, without stopping, he went on to describe his little games.

He would let me lie on his belly, my yard in the warmth of his thighs, his body in my arms, his throat in my mouth, or his breast, his shoulders, his armpits to be bitten at my will, and I might lie there, still, so still, with his legs held in mine, my hands under his thighs to guide my yard when it swelled, as swell it should, swell, swell, stiff, till all of me throbbed and I thrust and thrust, striving to pierce his thighs, thrusting 242 times fiercely and more fiercely, thrusting with all of me – then – suddenly – a little opening of the fat of the thighs to let the strong yard through, panting and spitting with joy. Such indeed was his power of giving joy that he would urge me on, even then, to thrust more, fifty times more, even through, and a second time spit deeper joy before my yard should tire. He, if I wished it so, would spit simultaneously. Or, if I preferred, would lie on me while I was resting and spit four times in twenty-two minutes of the clock.

This for the beginning of the evening. Then we could rest in each other's arms to recover breath for a little kissing and fondling. And he knew how to wriggle just a little all the time, flesh to flesh, entirely naked for the diversion of Signiori. Kissing, he thoroughly understood in every part, especially a certain kind of kissing in his patron's armpit, whose body he held in his arms, clasping his legs with his legs – kissing of a fury inconceivable, admirable for excitation. Next, he was ready to be rammed behind, spreading his knees as wide as they would go, and as for bounding meanwhile, well, I ought to see it, for truly he could bound (opening himself) so well that he would have the whole yard thrust among his hot interiors, till he himself was stiffened with it and the spitting took place in his throat. And also, as to spitting in the throat, let his patron but lie on the bed, legs hanging over the end, and he above would lie on the body,

VENICE LETTERS

breast to belly, arms in advance opening the thighs; and he would suck at his patron's yard with his mouth, but his own feet high on the bed head, his thighs also open, he would dangle his own yard to be sucked at will by his patron's lips till, both together at a signal, both might drink the juices of one another.

A little sleep, locked together, for an interval. Then, both being very hot, for the sake of coolness before sleeping for the night and to appease his patron's lust, he would extend himself across the bed, his legs hanging here and head and arms hanging there, his body and thighs ready to receive his patron. Let him mount. Let him ride. I stretched out with him to do with me what he will. And then a night of sleep in embrace. Who wakes first lies along and on the other, taking his fill of pleasure. Perhaps the patron wishes a little passage in the streets to take the air. We return and begin again. I shall always have new twists of my body for the Patron. We eat lunch. We spend the afternoon in bed. We eat dinner. Perhaps we see a kinematograph. Then another night, meeting together for diversion as before. In the morning early we wake and cling together before parting. And so to Venice. Sior, I pray you to try me. Only for affection (*pro affetto*) let me make you know what I can do. I said I couldn't afford it. Would I not then let him come to my palace. Any evening after five till six in the morning he was at the disposal of this Signiore. NO: I couldn't have him there; it was not convenient. Did he know of any place where we could go for an hour or so? It grieved him, but, No, not now. He had a patron, an artist, in Calle something on Zattere, also an English, who at 3.50 a day painted him naked on Wednesdays and used him for diversion then – but he could not take another patron there. I should think not, indeed. If I would go to Padova, he would pay his own fare. No. No. I was sorry. I was in despair. I would let him know when I could and then I most certainly would. Have some more wine. A thousand thanks but, no. Another cigarette. Twenty thousand thanks. So we came away.

He says that Peter and Zildo love each other and do everything to each other but to no one else, though he and Peter once had a whole summer night together on the lagoon in P's father's gondola. P. also is in much request among women but cannot spit more than twice a night. Whereas Amadeo has done it 8 times and vows that he could do 12 with a hot patron! Comments please.   R.

33

7

December 11, 1909.

Dear C.,

I changed the Order quite easily at a money-changers *without signing it* and got 6.25 for it, i.e. 2½d. more than its face-value. How this came about I do not know; and it is needless to inquire. But oh, my dear, my dear, if you only knew that each loan of this kind stamps me down deeper and deeper and more loathsomely into the mire – relieves me for the moment, but is worse than useless for setting me free and on my feet! This is not ungracious. I am indeed most grateful for your kind feelings to me. You are absolutely the only person in this world to whom I can speak openly and friendly. Imagine then how I value your friendship – and how anxious I must be to deserve it and to maintain it. And, *just because I have the most ardent desire to keep your friendship, which comes to me at a time when I have no other friend*, – I implore you to read and ponder what follows as earnestly as you can. I am certain that this state of things cannot continue. Why is it that I have had so many friends in the past, and now have lost them all? The reason is simple. They got tired. They liked me; and they pitied my penury; and they gave me little teaspoonsful of help. But friendship is only possible among equals. There must not be any money mixed up with it. And, by and bye, you also will get tired and bored and annoyed by the continual groans which I'm forced to emit, howling for a strong hand once for all to come along and haul me out of this damned bog and set me on my feet. It would not be such a very big thing, neither difficult nor unsecured. *I could give a first charge on my new book* ready in Feb., for two hundred sterling down and two pounds a week for six months. With that, I could instantly put myself in a decent position, secure all my property in proper management, and go on working like blazes at fresh books. For God's sake, make a violent effort then and get hold of some likely businessman to do this for me. That would be the act of a true friend; and you would have no more pain and infinitely more pleasure out of our friendship which has begun so extremely inauspiciously. I say inauspiciously for this reason – if you were an ordinary man, like C. or J.,[28] on seeing me shabby, miserable and poor, you would have done as they did and been civil and said good morning. That would have been natural. But, being one of ten thousand, you went a jolly sight further. The poverty and misery and shabbiness which were inauspicious enough to put them off, did not have that effect on you. But, it will, my dear, it will – unless we can change my inauspicious circumstances right soon. You'll get tired. And I shall lose a chance of keeping another friend . . . Now I know you're not the kind of man who does good deeds for the sake of a reward. So I'm sure you won't misunderstand what I'm going to say next. You say that you look forward to next Autumn. You also said, directly you got back to Falmouth, that you always seemed to get all the good things you wanted in a lump at the end of your holidays when you couldn't use them. Then *wouldn't it be wiser to make arrangements to have them ready for you at the beginning of your next holidays*, and not to have the trouble of so much fruitless hunting. Peter will be in the *carabinieri* by next Autumn, Zorzi (the Greek) in England, Amadeo and Zildo and Carlo much too big. But if I were free NOW, by the means described on the former page, I would have your place ready with suitable servants by next Autumn. And more – if I were free NOW, there wouldn't be any difficulty about putting my property in proper management and getting enough cash out of it to pay off the £260, and also, to bring Peter and Carlo to any place you liked in England for a month *whenever you pleased*. See that now. Think it over; and then strike out boldly.

I've written again to Eduardo. I'm convinced that he's frightened out of his wits. And, as I said, it's extremely unlikely that the address which he gave Cockerton will find him at all. 'Via 22 Marzo' simply means 'March the Twenty-second Street.' And he doesn't give his *number*. Now the number is most important: for, in Venice, it's not the streets which are numbered, nor the parishes, but the districts of which there are six. It's like numbering the districts of London. A London address, say somewhere in Victoria Street Westminster, if given in Venetian fashion would be 'Victoria Street 5795 Westminster'. Another in Paddington would be 'Praed Street 14523 Paddington'. And Eduardo's address ought to be 'Via 22 Marzo (let's say) 3615 San Moisè Venice'. It's the house number that's lacking;

and Heaven only knows how I'm to find it. However I've had another shot with a *post-card* now. And will report if anything occurs.

I'm glad you like my descriptions. Tell me, do they make you see, and feel, and give you pleasure, really? I particularly want to know: because writing is my trade, and I am always seeking to find out my faults and weaknesses so that I may improve them. Writing's a poor sort of job: but I want to get mine as perfect as I can. And it's only perfect when I succeed in exciting my reader, carrying him out of himself and his world, into my world and the things which I am describing. The newspaper critics (who are about as tedious a class of men as you can find anywhere) say that my writing is 'extraordinarily vivid'. But that's not good enough for me. It doesn't tell me what I want to know, viz. whether my writing makes my readers' imagination see and smell and hear and taste and feel what I describe. I'm afraid I made rather a failure of the Amadeo incident. But it was so utterly out of the common, even here – his quick hot chatter, all to the point, poured into my ear like a torrent – his feverish anxiety to give himself, every atom of himself inside and out, entirely away – his lightning-like exposure of his stock-in-trade, stripping in a flash, tossing his big, rosy, muscular nakedness backward – the wriggle, the stretching out of all, the instant of stiff waiting, the alluring grin – and then the quick recoil and covering up. What he would be like in use I tremble to imagine. The boiling passion of him was absolutely amazing. As far as I am concerned, I'm certain that a Saturday to Monday at Padua would simply be one long violent bout of naked wrestling and furious embracing so strengthening and invigorating to mind and body that I should be set up for a month. I'm not by any means a weak creature myself; and though I'm very slow to work up to a pitch, yet, when I am worked up I can behave quite terribly and not tire. And Amadeo is just ripe, just in his prime. I know that type so well. A year ago that day when he came to take the 3rd oar in my *pupparin*, he was a lanky uninteresting wafer. Since then, the work of dancing up and down planks with heavy sacks has filled him out, clothed him with most lovely pads of muscular sweet flesh, sweated his skin into rosy satin fineness and softness, made his black eyes and his strong white teeth and his mouth like blood glitter with health and vigour, and fired his passions to the heat of a seven times heated furnace. He'll be like this till Spring, say 3 months more. Then some great fat slow cow of a girl will just open herself wide, and lie quite still, and drain him dry. First, the rich bloom of him will go. Then he'll get hard and hairy. And, by July, he'll have a moustache, a hairy breast for his present great boyish bosom, brushes in his milky armpits, brooms on his splendid young thighs, and be just the ordinary stevedore to be found by scores on the quays. Oh Lord – and not to be able to devour his beauty so freely offered now! That's the sort he is. Do you know I'm convinced of this – there's a lot of lovely material utterly wasted and thrown away. Boys who *like* sporting with their own sex are rare. Oughtn't they therefore to be made welcome and carefully cultivated when they're found? And, isn't this a fact also? Given a boy, a fine strong healthy boy, who does actually enjoy the love of a male with all its naked joys, who burns for it, seeks it, flings himself gleefully into the ardent strivings of it with no reserve, with utter and entire abandon, offering himself a willing sacrifice or operating in turn with equal and greedy unreservedness, is it not a fact that such a one keeps his youthful freshness and vigour infinitely longer than the ordinary lad who futters the ordinary lass from puberty on? And isn't it also true that the passionate boy must have an outlet for his passion; and, if he (preferring the male) can't for whatever reason have what his nature prefers, doesn't he almost automatically sink into the arms of a female and instantly become 'man-like'. Look at Fausto. That Jew is a begetter of offspring. He certainly isn't a source of pleasure, pure pleasure, to his kind. He's young enough yet to be amusing, perhaps for ten minutes. But I defy anyone to regard him as a dainty morsel to devour, as a piece of sweet young flesh for the embracing of one's arms and thighs, as a lovely body panting with love to be hugged to one's own. And so I say with regard to all of the present set – unless they are used and cultivated *now*, they will flower at Easter, fruit at Midsummer, and be fallen by the Autumn. Of course there are others. But how to find them ready when wanted? – Now I must tell you about my typhoid boy and his brother. I think I mentioned the first to you, Bettamio by name. I used to go and see him every day when he had typhoid (caught at Castelfranco[29]) last August. We went a very long way *in words* on the road of love then. He was beautiful in bed, what I saw of him, which was not much, for his people were always present. But once we kissed hands. His father's a captain-engineer in the Navy. He lives with his mother (separated privately from the father on account of difference of temperament, but not divorced) and two brothers of 13 and 11 (he is 16) in a poor but very respectable way. When he got better, he took a clerkship at 7 fr. a week; and I used to walk home with him at night. Of course I don't go to his mother's house ever. (He was ill at an uncle's house.) A bachelor can't go to a semi-divorced woman's house. Well: we were very friendly. He is dark, tall, slim, straight, very sweet-spoken, with engaging manners and a charming way of fondling one's arms. In fact we had just got to the point when he would have been delighted to be kissed on parting. Kissing would have become habitual. And, a boy like that, although he does go occasionally to a bordel, would only have been too glad to learn the safer sweeter way. Well, one day he didn't keep an appointment. After that, for various reasons, I made no attempt to see him for some days. First, because I am easily offended: next, because I was desperately poor, miserable, and unable to take the next step, to do what I wanted, in short to go with him to Burano for a night and a day, say Sat. to Mond. where we could have slept together. And for several weeks, until yesterday actually, we neither met nor had any communication. We had no quarrel. I simply made no movement to avoid him, nor to see him because I hadn't the means to see him naked. And he made no movement to see me, no doubt because he was shy. Then, yesterday he called me up on the telephone, would I meet him that evening as usual, said very shyly and hesitatingly. I said that I would write. This morning at 8 I was rushing out to hear a mass (I've been in bed since my last to you[30]) when I ran bang into Bettamio. (He was exquisite.) He raised his hat and held out a nervous hand and began to explain. He had forgotten the appointment. 'Why have you left me alone?' Silence. 'I can't wait.' So I rushed on. I have just written him this:– 'I don't understand why thou hast saluted me on the street this morning. Either thou wishest to have me for your friend, or thou dost not. If, in truth, thou wishest to have me for a friend, why hast thou deserted me all these weeks? The appointment was that I might see thee in uniform (he's a Volunteer). I was at the Bridge of St Euphemia[31] from 6.30 to 8.30 and thou didst not come. Several weeks of silence followed. Thou hast not sought me, in person, or by letter, to explain or to excuse thyself. And now, after long negligence, thou treatest me as though I had offended thee. Thou makest me tired. I have not offended thee; but by thee I am offended, me, a friend ready to give thee my all. If any trouble or ill fortune prevented thee, why has thou hidden it from thy friend? Why hide anything at all of thine from him? Why dost thou not give me the frankness and the confidence and also the affection which I have given to thee, and which thou must give to me if thou wishest to have me for a friend. I have been ill in bed and am not able even now to come out at night to talk. Therefore, write, if thou desirest, from heart to heart.'

I think you'll agree that this is a pretty plain declaration which either will finish with him or will bring him to my arms. If the former, he is not worth worrying about. If the latter, Heaven send me means to *take him on the hop*. This will be from Sat. to Mon. next ensuing. I do hope it will come off; for I believe him capable of causing and enjoying ecstasies of pleasure. There is another reason also why I earnestly desire it: I have my eye on his brother (Gallieno or some such name) aged 13. When Bettamio was ill this youngster must needs have a day in bed in the same room too with a cold. He was quite naked and much too active to remain still, bounding about and scrambling across the room every now and then in an entrancing manner, manifesting fine and joyous thighs and a perfectly lovely little breast muscle extended to the shoulder. He is a lively creature with a sunny skin, hot eyes, chestnut locks, a big burning mouth; and likely by next Summer to be a bounding bouncing piece of virgin flesh well worth squeezing. I have an eye to the future you see. Oh pray do work hard for me now. I got a frightful cold directly after my last to you. The sunless cold of this windy stone landing is simply unspeakably atrocious. Consequently I had to go to my bed (one blanket) and heap my clothes on it. 'My way of treating a cold, dear Rolfe,' sweetly said the Dr 'is a sure but a hard one. Pray earnestly to God either to deliver you from it or to sanctify it to you and give you patience to bear it. This, with 8 days on pure barley water alone will do you good. After that, don't eat so much. Coffee and bread twice a day is what I recommend for your ordinary diet.'

So I prayed, and drank the beastly barley water, and now I take the filthy coffee and bread twice a day: and I've coughed so much and shaken myself so horribly over it that I can't cough any more but just sit up in bed trying to keep warm and write. But it's slow and wretched work. I've only been out once all the time. Oh my dear C. do for Friendship's sake, come to my rescue instantly. Here's Christmas close at hand. Is it to be my second in this miserable and hopeless impotence or the first of a new era? R.

N.B. On no a/c speak of Nicholson to me. He burned my papers out of sheer cowardice and spite. What about that photograph of two entwined? Do get the confession but first describe the confessor to me, age, appearance, condition, disposition, history.

8

December 28, 1909.

Dear F.,

A thousand thanks for your letter and the P.O's. The last have been a real joy: for they have enabled me to fee the Alphabet[32] and keep them in a good temper. These Venetians think such a lot of Christmas and the New Year that to let these festivities pass without the usual acknowledgements would have fatally injured future prospects. I told them that the tips came from you; and you would have chuckled to hear their comments. Piero was particularly touching. 'Sior, is it from the lord with the moustaches or from the [*erasure*]?' I said that it was from the lord with the moustaches. 'Ah,' says P., 'it goes well. That lord has a heart like his moustaches, of pure gold. May his soul sit on Mary Virgin's lap!' None of them [*erasure*]. They [*erasure*]. I can't get anything else from them but that: except that Carlo explains elaborately that G. threw him without warning. Piero and Zildo instantly asked for the favour of my company at a cinematograph. So we went. It was a beastly show: but the step was in the right direction. You simply have no idea what magnificent creatures they are, both huge, growing larger every day, Piero long and sinewy, Zildo long and muscular, fine upstanding figures both plump enough to damn a saint, and as hot as fire. And Zildo's slow sweet splendid smile. Lor!

My second postcard to Eduardo is quite unsuccessful. I haven't the faintest notion how to find him. I rather fancy that I passed him in this Campo[33] one evening at dusk, but am not sure. If I were decently dressed, and had a place to ask him to, I should stroll nightly in Piazza San Marco. If he is anywhere, he is sure to be there. But I'm convinced that he is frightened, and will take some finding and some management when found.

And my postcard to Bettamio also failed entirely. He hasn't said a single word. But I met his young brother – Saverio is his name – in San Trovaso. He took off his cap most politely and would have spoken: but I just nodded and passed on. The game to play in that quarter is to keep them at arm's length for the present. Later, when one is capable of doing anything it would not be a bad notion to cultivate Saverio at the expense of his brother. There's nothing wrong with the last, I'm sure, he's only very young and shy, and proud, and could be easily broken in, if one were not so helpless.

As for me, things have gone from bad to worse. I have never had such an unchristian Christmas in my life. Never! Neither beef nor turkey nor plum-pudding nor mince-pie have passed my lips, and I ADORE them all. Not a single soul said or sent a single Christmas word to me excepting the servants here and the boys. No, not one. That abominable Nicholson sent me a picture of a gondola (coals to Newcastle) and a verse out of Isaiah about affliction being for one's good. He has a talent for the inopportune which amounts to positive genius. – I don't think I have ever felt so utterly and hopelessly miserable before. Worse remains. Our dear pious Plymouth Brother of a doctor dismissed three of his six servants when I last wrote to you,[34] the man and two maids: and shunted on to me their work which I have been doing ever since. This gets me up at 5.30 to light fires, fill cisterns, work the cream-making machine, and get up wood for the stoves. It's devilish hard work. The wood comes in barges and is stacked in the cellar in logs. There are 2 kinds, one for kindling and the other for burning. And I saw the logs into shape, split the kindling into sticks with an axe and carry up stairs, about 10 basketsful a day, each weighing 140 lbs. That's the minimum. I wear a long blue blouse and am in fact a *facchino*. One reason why I am so infinitely obliged to you for the P.O's is that it enabled me to tip the three remaining servants. If I hadn't been able to do that at Christmas, they would have treated me as one of themselves; and their insolent familiarity would have become intolerable. As it is, though I wear a servant's livery and do a servant's work and chop my hands to pieces for lack of experience with the beastly axe, the being able to supplement my gently haughty demeanour with tips has so far saved me from undue annoyance. But, isn't it a dreadful shame? Of course my book is at a standstill. How can I possibly write when I'm toiling upstairs bent double with a load of wood, much less think out what I'm going to write with my mind raging in agony and disappointment? However, I have to do it for bread and a bed on a landing, and about 2 hours a day to myself. It's most hideous.

The arrangements for the moving are not quite completed yet.[35] There's some hitch about the house in Ventidue Marzo and another is under consideration on the Zattere. But they mean business: and I fancy will be out of this by the middle of Jan. I simply can't imagine what's going to happen to me. You are the only person I can look to. No doubt you'll have been able by then to get some one just to set me on my feet and give me a chance of getting myself clear of this appalling imbroglio. I know you'll worry your hardest and I haven't the least doubt that you'll succeed. Only the waiting, wasting time and chances is so horrible to bear.

N.B. Have you forgotten the photograph of two entwined which you talked of sending me. I fancy that a few things of that kind in one's pocket book would be an excellent way of educating some of the people here, especially the untried ones whom I have in view, who naturally would be the most satisfactory.

I hope you enjoyed Clifton. What do you do there? If I knew more about you I could write more to your taste no doubt, and if I had known you were going to Clifton I could have mentioned two in Bristol quite worth anyone's while.[36]

Now I must go and chop some more of that damned wood. The Dr is giving a Christmas Tree to 39 poor children and 75 adults whom he has attracted to his prayer meetings on Thursdays. It is to be down in that great hall of the palace which leads to the water-gate; and the amount of wood the furnace will consume for heating it simply would amaze you. I had already sawed and chopped and piled up logs about the size of a haystack: but the Dr came smiling by this morning: and 'Heap on more wood, the wind is chill,' 'It's a poor heart, dear Rolfe, that never rejoices,' and 'Ought we not to be thankful for the privilege of ministering thus to our loving

VENICE LETTERS

Father's less fortunate children?' says he. Ouph! I do feel so sick. For, not a whiff of the pine comes up my landing, and there's my book screaming for me to finish it. Oh, do send me some good news.

Ever – R. Please.

I must try to touch those senses of smell and touch and taste in my next. I could do it, I know, in a minute if I could refresh my own memory once or twice. Please. Please. Please.

1910

9

[POSTCARD] January 6, 1910.

Immediate need. Wire!

10

Same address. Thursday [? January 13, 1910].

Dear F.,
Oh my dear, my dear: I didn't mean that. For Heaven's sake let me explain.

I have been having a shocking bad time. This chopping and carrying of logs is beastly, not because I can't do it or have failed to do it – on the contrary, I have done and am doing it like a professional – but because it has completely stopped me from finishing my book. Nearly a month has been wasted already. Consequently I screeched on a postcard: but I didn't for a moment mean 'Send Money'. You amuse me, you know, by the way you chuck it about. It's perfectly admirable and most unusual. There's a girl in Harold Frederic's[37] *Illumination* whose views seem to be yours exactly. She says 'It is the one fixed rule of my life to obey all my whims. Whatever occurs to me as a possibly pleasant thing to do – straight, like a flash, I go and do it. It's the only way in which a person with means can preserve any freshness of character. If they stop to think what would be prudent to do, they immediately get crusted over. That is the curse of people with money: they teach themselves to distrust and restrain every impulse towards unusual actions: and so they get to feel that it is more necessary for them to be cautious and conservative and conventional than it is for others. I would rather work at a wash-tub than occupy that attitude toward my bank-account: I fight against any sign of it that I detect rising in my mind.'

What I meant was that it would be so nice to get things put on a firm basis now. Don't for a moment imagine that I distrust you or am disappointed if you fail a time or two. Oh no. I have absolute confidence in you. All you have to do is to keep on plugging away, and you're bound to bring it off sooner or later. I'll be as patient as you like and back up your efforts on my behalf with perfect hope and trust. What I propose to do with the wired 50^{38} is to keep it in hand and spend a little now and then in keeping the creatures in a good humour by a tip or a kinematograph now and then ... I can't spend your money on myself. It would look bad. One can't take alms from a man with whom one is on friendly terms or going to have business relations. See? So please, if you love me, go ahead and knock this damned brake off the wheel. Then you shall see me hum ...

I found these photographs of Carlo and Zildo. The clothed ones you might like to give to Tuke. I think the ones of Carlo rowing are very sweet. Pity he has but one ball. If you like them, I fancy I can scratch up some others. Oh Lord yes, by all means send me as many photographs as you can spare, specially of couples entwined. They will be most educative. And never mind about the Confessions being poor. Of course they will be poor, because they are not written by a trained writer. But let me see them all the same. It's the FACTS which I want. Give me the facts, and the personal emotions, feelings and experiences, and I'll guarantee to put them in a readable shape. So let me see the stuff anyhow. Then, if you like, let me correspond with the person through you. When I have some sort of a notion what he is like, and what his tastes are, and also his capabilities, I could set him an examination-paper to answer, which, I fancy, would produce some very explicit and unusual information. The point, of course, would be that he and I are and should remain perfect strangers to each other, and you alone would be between. In this way research and revelation of very secret matters indeed would be insured. You ought, however, to let me see a photograph of the person's person to help my diagnosis of him. Now try this ... Tell me, do you want a very nice Jew of 16? If so, I'll send you an address at Bristol ...

Being unable to go to Florence, or to enjoy any of my numerous opportunities here, I have been thinking a great deal about something Cocker said when I saw you. You both preferred the small, the 14 – while my preference was for the 16, 17, 18 and large. I have been trying to understand your preference, to find a reason for it, and I totally fail. This is why. *There is not enough of a little person for me to enjoy all of it.* It lies naked on its back. I stretch myself on its belly, my yard in the softness of its thighs. I clip it with my legs and arms: it hugs my body: and we begin to wrestle. But, where is its face? Where are the sparkling eyes, in whose depths I may see the ripple of pleasure? Where are the hot sweet lips which I may devour with mine? Buried under my breast and half suffocated. And I cannot thus enjoy the long long joys of contact, the delicious rests in struggling, the kisses and the vigorous renewals. But a big and lusty young body, like Gildo's or Amadeo's or Piero's, gives me all I want. The long muscular legs strain my thighs widely to clutch them. My yard thrusts through the cleft of their big thighs, my belly feels the heat and throbbing of their raging yard; and my body stretches to its uttermost, clutching their writhing clinging bodies large and soft and heaped with lovely muscles in my arms, to reach their rosy mouths, to breathe their burning soft sweet breath, to kiss wildly in the fight, to laugh and kiss their brilliant sparkling eyes and every inch of them within my reach, and to sink panting on their great white shoulders or to bite their gorgeous throats, breast to breast and heart to heart. Do you see? A soft little body is all very well to lie in one's arms all night: but it cannot give me furious joys. I want one long enough to be face to face with me while I thrust through its thighs, and strong enough to struggle and to give as much joy as I take. (Oh when? Oh when?) Do talk about this subject in your next. Regarding Cocker [*erasure*] ...

N.B. It was not I who said he was [*erasure*]. It was Piero and Carlo. I liked him very well. Ask him to write to me UNRESTRAINEDLY and I'll answer him as I only can. Yours, R.

P.S. Now I go back to my chopping, quite content with the knowledge that you are doing your very best for me in England all the time. You can't do more than that, and you can't be unsuccessful. I *will* it otherwise.

VENICE LETTERS
I I

[Begun] January 20, 1910
[and completed January 27]

This letter is going to be done in bits.

What amazes me is that, though you know so little of me *you do believe what I say, instead of discounting it or pretending to* MAKE ALLOWANCES AS EVERYONE ELSE DOES. Of course this makes it possible and even delightful for me to treat you with perfect confidence and to give you absolute accuracy; whereas to all the rest I naturally answer fools according to their folly, and omit to cast my pearls before animals which prefer acorns.

Here is a budget of news: (1) about Zorzi and Fausto: (2) about a row between Piero and Zildo: (3) about a league against Piero by Carlo and Zildo: (4) and how the last two went to the play at your expense and wish to thank you for it.

(1) Yesterday I had a surprise visit from Zorzi and Fausto. Zorzi is 'Giorgio' the Greek. They came to present their respects to me at the beginning of the year (fairly late) and to ask whether I could do anything for poor Fausto. He has been sacked from the Bucintoro (where I don't dare to go till I pay my arrears) for the winter and wants a job. These Venetians are devils about sacking their servants when they don't want them. Consequently, during the winter there are shoals of boys *simply starving for any kind of job*. I could put my hand on eleven at this moment, glad enough to do anything. Fausto looked very haggard and miserable. His face is hideous though his figure is admirable. I'm not by any means keen on him, though I can't help feeling ragingly wretched at not being able to help him.

Thanks to you I gave him a small tip and a cigarette and said I'd remember him if I heard of a job. *Oh for a little place, only a little place, of my own.* One could always squeeze in an extra, like this, at a pinch, now and then. Impotence to help others, poor devils, is damnable. But Zorzi – Zorzi, my boy is simply splendid. He grows upon one. I haven't seen him for a month or more; and yesterday he struck me straight in the heart with a loud yell. Such soft smooth flesh! Such a delicate rounded form, strong and subtle.

BARON CORVO

He's a slight little fellow of 17, *steered the Bucintoro eight to victory at the Olympic Games at Athens two years ago*, and speaks English with the most delightful hesitation. He has exquisite manners, is at school studying English, and comes to an antiquity shop in England next September. He came yesterday to assure me of his wish to serve me 'in any way, Signore, in any way'. I want most awfully to give him a job, after his school hours, and (if possible) from Saturday till Monday. *Oh for a place of my own, etc.*

(2) Piero and Zildo have quarrelled and parted. For more than a year now they have been lovers, working all day in Zildo's father's firewood business. Now Piero has no end of a tale about Zildo's infidelity! I'm inclined to fancy that Zildo has got to know of Piero's very occasional lapses towards the Fondamenta Osmarin, and has made the single experiment of going there too, all on the sly.

Zildo is so grave, so sweetly modest, that he would be certain to make his first experiment all alone and try to keep it secret. But he is so huge, so bursting with young vigour, that I suppose he simply had to break out in a fresh place somewhere. He himself admits nothing; though he still speaks most lovingly of Piero saying only that the latter suddenly and slightly unreasonably became *'fastidious'* (*el ga presso una fastidia*) *and bounded away in a rage.* Piero is almost incoherent with fury.

Zildo, according to him, is a traitor and an infidel, black, and indeed, almost Turkish! Beyond that, he gave me no details. And one only has the fact that he, Peter is out of a job, pinched and wan with want of food, bunched up and shivering with cold, hanging miserably about on the Zattere in want of work. *Oh, my dear, my dear, if only I had a little place of my own* – what's enough for one is enough for two. If I had it, and Piero, I'd pick his brains and write such a book as never yet was sold in Paris at 25 francs a copy, illustrated, oh yes, illustrated.

The part that I don't quite like is that Zildo's father has given Piero's living to Carlo and that Carlo and Zildo are what Zildo and Piero were till a fortnight ago. Also, there is no doubt but that Carlo rather rejoices in supplanting Piero. I don't quite approve of it. C. always had a living, a poor bare one, it's true, at his father's traghetto. His father and three brothers all had gondolas, and he is the youngest. But the unfortunate Piero is the oldest of about a dozen and his father can't possibly help him. His father actually has

12 sons and three daughters, all alive. I've seen Carlo and Zildo careering about the City with a boat full of fire logs many times. And imagine the chagrin of hungry Piero, who of course sees more of them than I do, living as he does on the very canal where they start from and return to every day!

I believe also that Zildo has taken Carlo on as concubine. Nothing else can explain Piero's shocked horror. My own consolation is that I can't believe the connection will last long. Carlo is a dear little dog; but he is incorrigibly liable to lapse into carelessness (which will lose him his job) and he's of luxurious tastes (so the wood sores and broken chilblains which I see covering his hands and wrists will be more than he can endure for long), and besides I know that he has in him the seeds of a born traitor who is congenitally incapable of being faithful to anyone for long.

(Here I go again – 25 Gennaio Jan.)

I had a word with Carlo that day 20 Jan. when I met them on the Fondamenta. Zildo left us together while he carried a load of logs into a house up an alley, leaving Carlo to mind the boat. 'How do you like sleeping with Zildo?' says I, abruptly. 'Sior, *e molto pesante – Sir, he is very weighty* and ravages me in his pleasure for an hour, suffocating me.' 'And you?' 'Twenty, thirty, forty thrusts through his sweet mountains, and then goodnight in his arms.' Zildo came back and both their eyes glittered like blazes. The simple little devils that they are!

And now I've got some real news for you. I had poor dear Piero all to myself yesterday morning on the Fondamenta Nuove. I was snatching a walk and met him on his daily hopeless tramp for work. (Lord, how my heart does bleed for him.) I gave him five francs *from you* and took him to a trattoria and filled him with polenta and wine. Then I picked his brains for a good hour; and found out everything. It's frightfully funny – even delicious. His word for Zildo, Zildo's conduct, manners, thoughts, words and works, is 'brutto' – *ugly*. Nothing worse than that. But 'UGLY!' And the facts are these.

Those two loved each other and '*the Paron*' (the last being me). And they agreed together to love no one but each other, and '*the Paron*' *of course might do with them just what he pleased, at his pleasure.* This agreement was made last summer. Piero accordingly gave up going to the Osmarin, and devoted himself entirely to Zildo till I should be ready for them. And, on New Year's Day, Zildo slips off secretly to the Osmarin *with Carlo* – (the insult to Piero of that, Carlo being an outsider!) – and enjoys five girls, one after another, stark naked and in broad daylight from 2 to 4 p.m. And Carlo followed on. 'Oh, what ugly creatures there are in this world!' comments poor Piero. (But imagine the joys of those girls over those two lusty and till then virginal ruffians!)

Piero found it out at night when Zildo had nothing to give him. He says that he couldn't sleep and took his clothes and went home.

Whereupon Zildo takes Carlo in his place; and those two have resolved not to risk disease but to be content with each other. 'So Sior, you see me friendless now' the piteous Peter ended. 'No, no,' I hastened to say, 'I am your friend always!' Whereat he burst into tears and began to kiss my hand. Oh my God, what a time I had to calm him. I was at my wits' end. At last, to gain time, I told him to meet me at the same place tomorrow and meanwhile I would try and think about something. But what to do I really do not know. If only another letter comes from you all would be well. At least I could give him a day's pleasure.

January 27.

Now I'm going to make you sit up. First of all I see that I've got this letter rather mixed, so I will finish it off as I began it, with number 4. I told you that I had tipped Zildo and Carlo in your name. Two days after they wrote hideous picture postcards saying that they had been to see Cavalleria and Pagliacci at the Rossini Theatre and thanked you for the pleasure of your gracious gentility. Very well. That ends that.

Now about yesterday. It appeared to me that the time was come *to break out of all caution and prudence. So I did, as thoroughly as you please.* Peter met me as agreed on Fondamenta Nuove. I explained to him exactly how I stood as to money, and I offered to give him all I had left of yours for his needs, or else to take him out for a day's pleasure.

If you could have seen how he beamed on me! He instantly chose the last. 'My pleasure is to be with my Paron,' he said. Fancy a great big boy of seventeen being as sweet as that! And he took

VENICE LETTERS

my bag – I had a satchel full of papers for the sake of looking business-like – and declared himself at my disposition. So we took the steamer to Burano where we lunched on beef steaks and cheese and wine, not at the inn you went to but another up the street. Lord, how he wolfed. It was a fiendish day – snow all night and the snow at Burano a good yard deep and still snowing.

While lunch was preparing I buried myself in my papers, asking questions of the landlord as to population, depth of water in canals and so on, and making notes for my book. While we lunched I had a scaldino of charcoal placed in a bedroom to make it comfortable for my siesta.

Then Piero and I went upstairs. I never saw anyone slip out of his clothes as he did – like a white flash – he must have unlaced his boots and undone all his buttons on the way up. Then he turned to me. He was scarlet all over, blushing with delight, his eyes glittered and his fingers twitched over my clothes with eagerness. As for his rod – lawks! As I came out of my guernsey he flung himself back on the bed, across the bed as he knows I like it, throat up, ankles crossed, thighs together and body expectant.

The clutch of us both was amazing. I never knew that I loved and was loved so passionately with so much of me by so much of another. We simply raged together. Not a speck of us did not play its part. And the end came simultaneously. Long abstinence had lost us our self-control. He couldn't, simply couldn't wait his turn, and we clung together panting and gushing torrents – torrents. Then we laughed and kissed, rolled over and cleaned up and got into bed to sleep, embraced. His breath was delicious. He pressed his beautiful breast and belly to mine and our arms and legs entwined together. So we took a nap.

I was wakened by a gentle voice 'Sior, Sior, Sior, with permission!' And his rod was rigid and ready. I took him on me. 'Slowly, and as hard as you like' I said. Oh what a time we had. He took me at my word splendidly and laboured with the sumptuous abandon of a true artist, straining his young body to his very utmost but holding himself in control prolonging the pleasure for the pure joy of it. As he writhed, I became excited in my turn and rolled him over to do with him; and close-locked we wrestled, how long I don't remember but I know that presently we were both gasping for breath and as rigid as ever. For a few minutes we lay side by side, hugging, laughing, devouring each other's lips and each trying to clip the other's thighs with his own. Then we began again, more fiercely than ever, and finished the matter. '*Oh, che bel divertimento!*' says Peter, squeezing me as we spouted – 'Oh, what a beautiful diversion.'

We took the 5.30 steamer to return to Venice. On the way he was most affecting. What a lover that boy is. He said that Zildo was nothing in comparison with me, that of all the pleasures he has taken, nothing has ever equalled this afternoon. As for the girls, let Zildo and Carlo take evils from them. They were 'ugly', and never had he believed that it could be as good as it was. Would I command him to come to my palace to serve me? No, that was impossible; when I was able to take a little apartment of my own, he should come and live with me. When? I did not know. Pray Sior, let it be soon. I asked whether he would serve if you came here. He blushed; 'I am the servant of the Paron and will be obedient always; but Sior, I pray to sleep sometimes in your arms.' His word for action is 'unlock'. He said that my key unlocked him most easily; if I wished him to try your key he would do his very best most willingly. But would I teach him to speak English so that he might surpass that ugly Carlo.

I got out my papers and made a little book, in which I wrote some Italian words with their English equivalents, like this:

Stupido sciocce – siliful (i.e. silly fool)

and numbers up to twenty and a few other words. He sat and learned them by heart, taking no end of pains. You can't think what a beautiful creature he really is, young, strong as a horse, slim and lithe and supple as a serpent, magnificently virile, with soft downy skin and firm hot flesh sweet as a baby's.

I asked him about sucking. No, he had never done nor had it; but gladly would he from me. Did one drink? Yes. Ah, what a beautiful diversion! So you see what joys are in store. And as to posterior treatment, he pronounced it 'ugly'. Zildo had done it once in the night and Peter had beaten him for being so 'ugly', i.e. brutto. How, he asked, could kisses of lips take place that way, kissing being part of the diversion of 'unlocking'. Dear thing!

When we parted I gave him the last two francs remaining to me and promised to write to you at once. This is the first chance I've had. And while I've been writing enclosed came. I thought you'd like to see it, so I translate it literally. Isn't it delicious?

God knows what's going to happen to me. There's some delay about the Doctor's moving which I don't understand; so I still stick on here. But I can't possibly move for the better on my own account in any way, nor do any new work, nor finish any old as things are. Don't think me impatient. I know you're doing your best and leaving no stone unturned for me and I'm quite content to leave it at that. Of course I'm awfully grateful. That you know. But you just wait and see how grateful I can be, tangibly, when once I'm free to make use of my powers. I think I shall surprise even you.

N.B. *I really think I'd risk starting on my own with £50, if that could be got in the meantime, and the £200 and a weekly allowance a little later.* I fancy it would be safe. Anyway, though my only hesitation is on account of seeming too sanguine, *I do most earnestly yearn to finish off this damned book and float it* and get on with a new one. It's a waste of time to chop the Doctor's logs when I ought to be writing.

Do write oftener.　　　　　　　　　　　　　　　　　　　R.

I send two photos of Piero taken last year at the wells in the Civic Museum. He wore that uniform when in my service. Do send me as many photos as you can spare.

12

February 10, 1910.

Dear C.,

Thanks for your letter. I was getting dreadfully alarmed about your health. It is a great relief to know that it has not suffered under the strain of the election or the weather. Here we have been having an abominable time, and the last night of the carnival was simply a torrential downpour which ruined everything. I saw nothing of the carnival myself, having other affairs to attend to all the time.

The Carnival of Venice has been going down for some years; but this year an effort was made to restore it to something of its old distinction. I'm told that the masked ball at the Fenice was really wonderfully beautiful and the price of the tickets (1.50 each) kept it quite select and free from undesirable people.

Besides that a lot of nobles gave Dancing Teas and they say that H.R.H. The Duke of the Abruzzi (who has just been made Commandant of the Arsenal) danced like an Archangel. This I had from two extremely pious princesses, who said that his performance was so beautiful that they followed him from one palace to another simply for the pleasure of seeing him.

I'm very sorry to hear of your business difficulties. Personally, you know, I am convinced that it is *not sound policy to work with old or doubtful or untested machinery or in unsuitable surroundings. No one can produce satisfactory goods when production is carried on under difficulties, and to trust to luck is simply rashness.*

I believe, indeed I know, that the only way to attain success is by working on modest lines with discretion and concentration, leaving nothing to chance. My own difficulty is merely want of capital, and a capable partner. I have a fair field, the place, the most up-to-date machinery thoroughly tested and proved sound, and I have a certain amount of stock ready for market, and a market found ready for it. All that is necessary is the capital and the partner. With these *the quiet and secure development of the concern would proceed as it were automatically.*

I wonder whether you would care to consider the question of joining forces. I think we could work together amicably and for our mutual advantage. In any case you know that I utterly refuse to engage in any enterprise of which I have not thoroughly thought out all the details and foreseen the successful conclusion. This may be slow; but it has too the merit of being sure. Think over the idea. Meanwhile, as I say, I am at a standstill and the gear is getting rusty, so that any help you can give towards oiling the wheels will be thankfully accepted until we can set affairs in motion.

Many thanks for the picture. It is not the one I expected. You spoke of a picture of two hounds fighting and that is the one I want to see. This one is not bad, but looks a lazy dog, and you know that dogs in action are what I collect. What is the age, pedigree and condition of this one?

Regarding the candidate for examination, to whom am I to send papers? I suppose he offers practical experiments as well as theory. It would be useful to know where he has studied and for how long, whether he took up the subject of his own unaided choice, and whether he really means to pursue it. With this information before me I shall know what standard of papers will be suitable, and meanwhile any information I can give is at his service if he will write directly to me in definite terms.

By the by I ought to add this:– I'm taking for granted that the candidate is quite serious and earnest about his work. I am willing to give him all the help in my power – but he must clearly understand that I am far too busy a man to waste time over anyone who has not a consuming interest and wishes to improve himself.

I judge that the candidate would not present himself for examination if the case were otherwise; and one will be able to see from his answers what his present state of knowledge is and in what direction his future studies may best be directed. Anyway, first let him write to me at some length giving full particulars, and this without delay. Please quote my words to him.

There has been a row with Zorzi, who is violently enraged because I wouldn't lend him my red smock to masquerade in at the carnival. Poor Piero is still out of work and frightfully haggard. He came blushing yesterday asking for a loan of 8 francs for a pair of boots, his own being the merest mockery, worn to the ground and bursting. It grieves me to the heart to be only able to give him another pair of my own which can't possibly last him more than a week longer. I haven't seen any of the others since I last wrote.

As a matter of fact I've only been out of the house once since then. I went to look at the sweetest apartment you can think of. If you are inclined to join me it would be well worth thinking of. It is a top flat of a palace on the widest canal running round the square of San Giacomo del Orio close here. It is quiet and retired, though within touch of all centres. There is a water-gate with a store and cellars on the ground floor and a private entrance in the alley. The flat consists of four good rooms, kitchen, W.C., a long corridor and two big attics over. Besides these, the end room opens on to a *terrace or roof-garden*, properly railed and posted for canvas awnings.

And the situation is splendid. Every room has all the sun of the day because the place stands high and apart from the surrounding buildings. Immediately below is the square and church of San Giacomo, more than 1,000 years old and wonderfully quaint. And the view on all sides is all over Venice, to the Alps on one side and the Lido on the other. And the rent is 60 francs a month without any taxes. It's simply ideal, but I'm afraid it will be snapped up if I don't make up my mind quickly about it.

I think that's all for to-day. The weather's vile. Everything's as bad as it can be. Do write by return for I can't get on till you do.

R.

13

[No place or date]

I'm sorry (or glad, whichever you please) to say that I totally disagree from you when you say that I ought to understand why it is not easy to reply by return of post when you have no good news to send. I don't understand at all. My dear man, it seems to me that when you are ill or worried or in trouble, that is just the very time when you most want consolation and amusement which a friend can give. I know that's how it is with me. And I know also how difficult it is to find a friend willing and proud to share one's miseries.

However, you needn't be afraid of me. I've got so many of my own that the addition of yours will make no difference. Besides, that you should think me worthy to share your ills is, to my mind, a mark of esteem and confidence so marked that it will go a long way towards relieving me of my own troubles. This isn't mere talk, I mean it literally. So pour out all your worries without fear. I not only don't object, but I implore you to do so.

Don't be a bit afraid of me. I'm discreet and safe and sympathetic, and so betimes it is given to me to say an illuminating word or two . . . And, you know, you've freely let me tell you my own annoyances; and you can't refuse to be as friendly to me as I am to you. Now can you?

It occurs that you may perhaps be afraid of my disappointment about the long delay in finding a partner. Don't make that mistake. I'm not a damned fool. I'm philosopher enough to know that you do what you can; and I don't expect you to do more. So put that off your scrupulous chest, please.

I'm sorry to hear about the source of your income. You've never told me yet what that source is. All I can say, then, is that when you get sick of things there, you'd better scratch up what you can and come to me. I'll share myself and my all with you most gladly, even to the uttermost. There isn't the slightest reason why we shouldn't do extremely well, beginning modestly by ourselves and taking on suitable machinery as we are able. Far better a modest certainty than dangerous and worrying rushing into speculative uncertainties. That game is never worth the candle.

And you have my commiseration also about your health. Influenza is infernal. Luckily we don't have it here; though of course we have our annoyances. Let me know how the cough goes. I always gorged 'Owbridge's Lung Tonic' when I had coughs in England. I've been in bed for the last month myself. It's the only place where I can keep from freezing as I write.

Of course, I go to mass on Sundays and once I went to Burano for a day; and of course I get up to do my damnable wood work and cream separating. But otherwise I creep in bed and get warm: and curse because I haven't got a boat in which to take decent exercise. You must please realise that a boat isn't a luxury as in England. It's a necessity. One is absolutely paralysed without it. *As a matter of fact, the possessor of a decent boat can bite his thumbs at misfortune.* He pays the municipal tax, but he needn't pay house-rent. He can live in his boat and do his job there quite well and be utterly independent of all and everybody. Mark that well, please.

I haven't had any communication from the candidate for examination yet. Please send him my name and address and tell him to write freely, giving the information asked for in my last. I am most anxious to get to work with him at once and to treat his subject quite fully. That is why I say that perfectly open communication between us is essential as a preliminary. Is he serious? (That's most important; because it's no use fooling with examinations unless he really means to pass them and to benefit by taking a little trouble to pass them.) So let's begin, instantly. *Meanwhile, send me what he wrote you.*

This doctor makes me sicker than a cat with his text chopping. I'm sure it's a form of mania. It appears that for the last six months he's been drawing his babies' money out of the bank to give to 'Recommended Christians', generally Germans, who go about the city raving drunk and chanting flat hymns or spiritual ditties. Consequently he's now selling his books and furniture bit by bit and his angry wife has to sell her dresses for food!! Fact! There was the devil of a row about the babies' money.

He smiles blandly and says that he's *laying up treasure in Heaven.* Did you ever hear such a b. fool? So I got in a rage and banged him on the snout (pink) with some other texts – 'the children ought not to lay up for the parents, but the *parents for the children*', and 'if any man provides not for his own, and *especially for those of his own house,* he hath denied the faith and is worse than an infidel'. But if you think that floored him, you're mistaken. These text-choppers never are floored, because they only take as much of their blooming Bible as is necessary to prove their own beastly biblidolatrous theories, and shut their heads against the rest. They make me tired. But the situation is very serious, though. Very.

I haven't seen anyone all this time. It's a great nuisance because when one wants to get to work, it will be all to do over again. However, I don't mind, if you'll only treat me fully and frankly as a friend who is ready to do anything for you in his power. Here's another text for you – 'Two are better than one'. Write, and make the candidate write.

By return.

No pictures have come yet. Can you see to this for me?

[*During most of the eight months Rolfe spent as a guest of the van Somerens he was engaged in writing his novel* The Desire and Pursuit of the Whole. *Early in 1910 he informed his hostess that he had almost completed his new book. She had asked him repeatedly to allow her to see the manuscript of this 'romance of modern Venice', as it is subtitled, but he had always firmly declined, telling her that she must wait until it was published. One day, however, Rolfe relented, on the explicit understanding that Mrs van Someren should say nothing of what it contained to her husband.*

This book, covering the period of Rolfe's first 15 months in Venice, is a romance liberally sprinkled with biting satire which castigates many of the prominent British residents of the city. It also chronicles the author's quarrels and intrigues, and almost every page contains a scurrilous reference to, or shameful libel on, one or another of the van Somerens' friends or acquaintances.

VENICE LETTERS

The respectable doctor's wife had not read very far when she told Rolfe she had seen quite enough to displease her. He thereupon entreated her to read just one more chapter. Reluctantly she agreed, only to be further outraged by yet more vicious caricatures of her friends. Mrs van Someren then informed Rolfe that in view of what she had read she felt fully justified in repudiating her promise. Thus, on the Doctor's return that evening, she told him of the contents of the manuscript. When he learned how his hospitality had been abused, he immediately gave the author the choice of either deleting the offensive passages in the book, or leaving the house. For a man of Rolfe's temperament there could be no compromise. Without hesitation 'he retorted he allowed nobody to dictate to him what he should write or not write, and he would leave to "starve on the streets of Venice"' (Ivy van Someren, 'Baron Corvo's Quarrels', Life and Letters, February 1947). The following day – March 5, 1910 – he took himself and his few belongings to the Bucintoro Rowing Club where, for a while, he rested by day, sleeping in one of the club boats by night, or wandering on the shores of the Lido.]

14

[TELEGRAM] Venice.   March 5, 1910.

Homeless penniless wire money British Consul Rolfe.

15

[POSTCARD]   Sunday [March 6, 1910].

Row with pious doctor, and left house on Saturday. Ate last on Friday evening. Walking all night on Lido beach beyond Excelsior. Often questioned by police who are on watch to see that no one evaporates salt from the sea. Say that one is a writer studying the dawns. So far satisfactory. But the cold is piercing and two nights have made me stiff as a post. Told Consul Saturday and asked him to wire to you. Something must be done. But spirits and determination undimmed. Letters to Consulate.

16

[POSTCARD]
286 Calle Larga San Marco,[39] Venezia.   March 31, 1910.

Instant need: but prospects better. Book finished. One copy gone to America. English offer to serialize it also, which means fees from two sources.[40] *Also* offer from Eng. firm to publish *The Weird*,[41] one of two MSS stolen by H.P.G. These improve security. Now make effort to finish things. Have begun new book.[42] *Last d.* Violent snowstorm all day. Would you like negative of Venice snowy?

17

April 5, 1910.

Dear F.,

Pen exhausted so please excuse pencil. A thousand thanks for your letter and enclosures. *The former is like water in a thirsty land.* You can't think how horrible it is not to have a soul to talk to. Look here; don't think that I blame you the least little bit. You never led me to expect anything and consequently I am not disappointed. What I admire (because they are so like my own, which I admire immensely) are your pluck and perseverance in keeping on through one failure after another. Nothing can beat a man in the end who keeps on long enough.

For my part I am going on as long as I can wag a little finger and I'm greatly helped in this determination by the knowledge that you're doing the same on my behalf, undismayed by rebuffs.

Things are quite unaltered. Quite. Except, as my postcard told you, I'm better off in the sense that I've got a new book finished and all my own, over which no one has any rights but me. All that's wanted is to realise on it and that can't be done without means. I've sent one copy to America: and shall hear of it in about three months at earliest. And I've got an offer to serialise it in England, which means that I must make another copy (2 months work) from the first draft, but this would mean cash on delivery of each chapter if only I had a chance of being able to finish the whole.

VENICE LETTERS

And then again there's the third offer which I've had for *The Weird*, written 2 years ago, stolen by Pirie-Gordon. My agents have a lien on this so I wrote and told them of the offer and said that if they would come to some terms with me I would let the book be published, so that we could both make a little money.

I gave them to last Sunday to decide, and they haven't even answered; so I am posting with this my refusal of the publisher's offer. (So far for facts. The following is conjecture. I've only refused a publisher's offer once before, but the result was that he instantly conceived an imperious desire for the book and *doubled his offer*. In the present case this may happen or it mayn't. One never knows.) You see Barnard and Taylor have been told so many silly lies by Pirie-Gordon, who's an important country gentleman and swaggers enormously, that they've put confidence in him and don't believe a word I say. Well, naturally I won't submit to that, under any circumstances; and all I do is to string them up with blind and naked fact from time to time, as in the present instance, and make them suffer for their unbelief. They think that if they sit long enough on the goods they've grabbed of mine, someone else will get me out of my pickle, please; but Barnard and Taylor shan't make a penny either out of my past work or my future unless they are the ones to get me out of my pickle.

It's awfully good of you to offer to see them; but it wouldn't be any good. All one can do is to keep on, as I do, when occasion serves, banging away at the same old cry – 'Render accounts of your 6 years mismanagement and let's make a new arrangement; till you do, all your liens shall be worth the price of waste paper'.

The landlord of the Bellevue has taken the *Clock Tower in the Piazza*. It is full of workmen altering the interior into a hotel. (My dear, the front windows have quite the loveliest view in the whole world.) He has given me an empty attic here to sleep in, and carpenters and painters and stonemasons and plumbers and water-closet makers walk over me day and night. I never was so dirty in my life, and having no boat and no privacy whatever I can't even go to bathe. Food also is a problem. I do with as little as ever I can and am delightfully thin and weak. Today I shall have a bath and eat and drink a litre of wine with Peter. Then back to 1d a day of bread till things change.

I have had several long talks with the landlord. I think he sees now that I am honest and no particular fool, and he isn't at all ferocious. But he's a man of one idea and I can't drive any others in to his head. He wants a guarantee. He keeps on saying 'You want clothes and a little good living and convenience for doing your work. Get me a guarantee and I'll find all the money you want'. And I say 'Oh, you make me tired. Ask me something possible'. Yah!

As soon as I got yours I rushed out to buy a packet of tobacco at that place on the Mole, where one is who is very willing. And on the way back who should I pass but Bolck (the first time since you left). He was frightfully funny. So funny that I shrieked with laughter out loud in the streets. He went on quickly with his head down just like a naughty child! I'll certainly speak if I meet him again. Do let me hear again from you at once.

I have a whole budget when you are ready to hear it of news old and new. Meanwhile, you see how I am.   Ever yours, R.

Nando Violo.

18

[POSTCARD] Venice.   April 15, 1910.

I told you that I was refusing offers of publication and serialization of *The Weird of the Wanderer*. B. and T. have a lien on it and I'm not going to let them make a penny while they withhold my accounts for two years and do not secure to me a share of my own work. Well: the result of the above refusal has been to produce this morning a new and better offer from the same publishers for the same immortal work. (I've never been asked twice to reconsider a refusal. It means that the publishers are CERTAIN about success . . .) Well: I've told this to B. and T., warning them that I shall refuse this second offer Apr. 23 unless I have good reasons otherwise. Here is additional security, though, for the partner who is to take over obligations and assets from B. and T. and manage them properly.

Things are getting terrible again here. That can't be too strongly realised. Horrid cough which will certainly become phthisical if I don't get exercise soon. Please keep things going. I told you what the man here said about the guarantee. Oh yes, here's more news

VENICE LETTERS

about the finished Venetian book. Have got an offer from England for serialization. Have also got the chief publisher here, Ongania, to ask publishers of my last 2 books to publish English edition while he issues Italian edition. This is [in] addition to America. But, you understand, nothing can be done till B. and T. are cleared away. I won't consent to their having another 1d. Have got Press ticket for Tarnowsky Trial here. Amazing![43]

Write. Write. Write.

19

[TELEGRAM] April 22, 1910.

Telegram received from British Consul Venice requesting you may be informed that Fr Rolfe is dangerously ill and penniless at the Hotel Belle Vue Venice. Foreign Office, London.

20

[POSTCARD]
286, Calle Larga San Marco, Venezia. May 12, 1910.

Left hospital yesterday after bronchitis, pneumonia, heart. Last Sacraments, due to exposure and privations of past year. Doctors (Italian) say I am the strongest man they have ever seen, otherwise nothing could have saved me: but now so weak that I cannot even walk 20 paces. Have absolutely no one to look to but you. Implore substantial and immediate help while I try to pick up dropped threads. Affairs look absolutely hopeless: but my courage remains untouched. If I can feed up I may rest and recover strength and lost ground. Have had exactly same illness as late King and say with him 'My back is against the wall and I will go on to the end'. Help please, quick. (34 minutes to write this.)

BARON CORVO

21

June 6, 1910.

Gildo and Carlo,[44]

Many thanks. I taste tobacco at last. Everything is at a standstill. I am stronger: but have had no rest or convalescence at all. Cough persists and top of lung isn't clear yet. This of course is due to getting no fresh air or exercise, of any kind, ever.

Barb.[45] has taken me in, given me a den on ground floor looking into alley, invaded by rats and grub with the staff. In return I have given him lien on new book. But the two copies of it are here: because there is no tin to send them to publishers. The MS. of a book is heavy and the postage is 4.25. I also have grubbed up MSS of 2 other books of mine, *Nicholas Crabbe* and *The One and The Many* which also are here, idle.[46] (By the bye, in connection with the idea that I am idle – please consider that I have invented and written every word of *The Desire and Pursuit of the Whole* FIVE TIMES since last July – $148,900$ words $\times 5 = 744,500$ words!!!)

I can't take walks because of boots and clothes. Nor can I bathe or row without boat. We have had blazing hot weather without a drop of rain since May 3. Gondolas and topos *can't* be had for L. 50 a day, sandolos are getting L. 30 a day easy. The place is simply crammed. The King is coming in the middle of the month.[47] I don't think you understand that Venice from Apr. till July is besieged by people who live on their fortunes, specially Russians and Americans. From July to October, the people who come belong to the salaried classes who take an annual holiday. The amount of money going begging just now is amazing. I see a lot of it here. The rooms on the Piazza are auctioned and never get less than L. 45 a night! In Aug. you can have one with balcony for L. 10.

Your last two letters have been disappointing. So reserved. I want news and I want to give news. Say when.

Yes, Consul wired my Brother.[48] He sent 2nd hand introduction to Armenians.[49] They couldn't do anything. That's all. It is naked truth that I have no one to look to but you, even for means to grub on.

VENICE LETTERS

22

June 30, 1910.

Dear F.,

I'm sure you don't realise how cruel this long neglect is. It has just hung up every chance I had. My new book is still here because I dare not begin to send it round the publishers without a permanent address to send it from. I've lost two offers for serialization also. And I have had to refuse the offer for *The Weird* because I haven't the means to secure my rights in it previously; I mean, if I let it be published as things are, B. and T. will instantly scoop the profits and give me nothing, for my own work, – I'm not only powerless and doing nothing, but *I'm expecting every day to be put in the street again.* People here have left off speaking to me, don't even say good morning. The fact is B. is tired of seeing how powerfully powerless I am.

Meanwhile Peter has ruined himself for life. He has been 30 days in the Civil Hospital with syphilis and was discharged on Monday as 'incurable'. He looks 70 years old and isn't 20. That is what comes of being unemployed. Had I a boat he would have been healthily working and earning a handsome living for both. It's simply heart-breaking. Why don't you write, anyhow?

23

July 11, 1910.

My Dear Man,

All I ask and beg and pray of you is that you'll write to me frequently and fully, and not leave me alone to get into dumpish moods when I take a pessimist view of everything. I entreat that you'll do this: for no one ever speaks a word to me here, nor can I get anyone in England to write to me, excepting on business, and only then with the greatest difficulty imaginable. The result of that, and of the life which I lead, is appalling. I'm *quite deprived of air, water and exercise* of any kind unless I go and walk about the island of Santelena⁵⁰ at 4 o'clock in the morning. I do that, as often as I can pluck up the energy: but I'm so hideously shabby that I daren't shew myself in the street by day. You know how crowded Venetian streets are. And after dark, the place swarms with people who are not respectable: and I am not going to be mixed up with them. Not once this summer have I been able to swim, merely because I have no means of getting out on the lagoon. I'm just pinned down to my room, a back room on the first floor of that narrow alley which leads from Piazza to Calle Larga, so close to the ground that I can touch the hats of the whores and drunks who roar there all night long, where never a ray of the sun has ever come, so dark that I can't see to write there on these brilliant days without the light on, and a playground *of rats* of which I have just trapped and drowned in the slop-pail the *thirty-sixth since July 1st! ! !* And the effect on me is that my hands shake like a palsy, my whole body tingles inside and has fits of giddiness, I can't lie on my left side because it stops my heart, and I cough with a chest filling up again. Heaven only knows what's going to happen. I don't.

I'm inclined to think that nothing can be done unless I make up my mind to have a jolly good public row. You see B. and T.⁵¹ made me assign them my policy; and, consequently, *they have everything to gain by my death.* While Pirie-Gordon, who has stolen my life-work and my goods, has the only evidence which I possess of B. and T.'s obligation to me. Therefore, if P-G. and B. and T. simply sit tight and let me die, B. and T. will scoop £450 and P-G. will have the manuscripts of two finished and four half-finished books,⁵² besides all my papers, and about £2,000 worth of clothes, curious books, curiosities, furniture – a life's collection of an expert collector, in short.

Now, if we could find that financial partner to take over my assets and obligations – or even if I could get a place of my own and means to live – I would recover all these things within a fortnight just by demanding them. It is merely my helpless condition which prevents that. And P-G. and B. and T. have made up their minds to take the fullest advantage of that condition. It isn't necessary for them to commit murder. *All they have to do is just to keep quite still while I die.*

Do you see?

Very good.

Now mark me well. I won't die, till I've had a good kick out all round. So this is what I've done.

I've written a detailed account to the Prudential of the means which B. and T. are adopting to kill me, keeping me without my promised income since Oct. 1908, refusing to exploit my works or to let me have them to exploit myself, reducing me to homeless penury which has broken down my magnificent health and given me one pneumonia and is in imminent danger of giving me another which I shall not be strong enough to overcome. I have definitely pointed out that B. and T. are to gain by my death, and have fully detailed the method they are adopting to procure it.

Also, I have denounced B. and T. to the Law Society, giving a full account both of their malfeasance of trust and the matter of the policy.

Also, I have denounced P-G. and B. and T. to the Publishers' Association as *thieves* of my work giving particulars of the works stolen so that no publisher will dare to issue them without my consent.

Also, I have denounced P-G. and B. and T. with full particulars to the Foreign Office: and have appealed for 'every assistance and protection of which he may stand in need' as required by my passport.

In short, I have been as libellous as I know how, in the hope that I may goad someone into bringing an action against me and giving me a chance of bringing the infernal injustice of which I am the victim to public notice. I have nothing to fear from exposure and it may be that this is the only way of getting justice done. However, we shall see.

All I beg of you is to keep up my spirits and put me in good fighting fettle with a little tobacco occasionally. Heaven bless you! I've been out and bought ten packets of 2d. cigarettes and a packet of bumph, and tomorrow I'll have my hair cut. There wasn't enough to buy a ream of paper and a new pen. I'm nearly out of the first and the second is a wreck after writing nearly seven million words. But they'll come later. Anyhow I'm a bit bucked up, thanks to you.

Isn't it simply frightful about poor Peter. His weight has come down 58 Chilogrammes to 15! ! ! I'm ashamed to say that I hardly dare look at him. It's no good for me to try to look at him as long as I can't do anything to help him. But with the first decent sum I get

I shall run him off to Solfatara[53] and give him a course of sulphur baths and plenty of good food to restore him. I think that if he could have a thoroughly good raking inside and out, and then be bathed in the sun and sea of the lagoon in a boat for a couple of months of summer, he might be made fit again to work. Of course he can't marry, ever. And I'm much afraid that they'll refuse him for the *carabinieri* when he goes for his military service next year.[54]

Now do tell me about everything.

Specially about your friend at Oxford.

I'm depending on you to keep me alive like this so that I shan't collapse till I've brought B. and T. and P-G. to book, if not this way then in some other. Do you want pictures?

24

August 1, 1910.

The Law Society and the Prudential Ass. say that they're unable to intervene. The Foreign Office and the Publishers' Ass. haven't answered. I am now sending a statement to the Public Trustee and the 'Athenaeum'. If I knew how to do it I should like to have the whole scandal discovered by the 'Daily Mail'.

I trapped the *fifty-fourth rat in my room* since June yesterday. Lack of mosquito nets has caused me to be eaten and consequently I've been more or less feverish for a week. Barbieri has begun to be very shirty and I'm expecting to be adrift on Aug. 5th or 6th again. So I warn you in time.

News from America that my new book *The Desire* and two others, with eighteen long magazine articles, have arrived and are being negotiated as quickly as possible. But do you know that it takes 23 days for a letter to get from here to New York and another 23 at least before you can get an answer? This of course seriously interferes with business.

Anything more tantalising than what has been happening about *The Weird* I find it impossible to imagine. As I think I've told you, I wrote 9/10 of that book to Pirie-Gordon's 1/10 and we were to share the profits half and half. I assigned my half to Barnard and Taylor. Pirie-Gordon has two typescripts of the book and my own manuscript of it and agreed to send them round the publishers till they found acceptance. I think he did at first. Anyhow my manuscript got into a publisher's hands and so back to me. But for two years P-G. did nothing whatever with his two typescripts and for two years B. and T. totally neglected to see that my work was being used. Then I, who am only a poor writer, and have no business ability, coughed horribly at these professionals and got to work myself with my own copy of the book. And of course a publisher instantly made me an offer of 4d. a copy royalty. I said to B. and T. and P-G. 'I've written the book, and I've found a market for it (which last was your business to do). And I'll accept the offer if you'll give a share of the profits to me who have done all the work, yours as well as my own'. They answered nothing. I refused the publisher's offer. He instantly raised it to 6d. a copy royalty. I told B. and T. and P-G. as before. They went on saying nothing. I refused 6d. The publisher instantly raised it to 8d. I advised B. and T. and P-G., got no answer, and refused 8d. Then, the head of the firm wrote me a personal letter, asking me to leave the matter open. I told B. and T. and P-G., got no answer, and after a month refused to leave the matter open. The result of that was another personal letter from the head of the firm ASKING ME TO NAME MY OWN TERMS FOR *The Weird* AND ASKING ALSO TO HAVE A SECOND BOOK FROM ME. I have told B. and T. and P-G., got no answer and am just refusing this offer also.

I've done all the work and I want some of the proceeds. Neither B. and T. nor P-G. shall have a penny from my brains and ability unless I make a halfpenny. In their greed at grasping at the whole, they'll fail to get anything at all. And their fortunate circumstances permit them to squat and look on at my desperate struggles in the hope of confiscating all my stuff in the event of my death. However, I'm trying to prevent that by announcing beforehand what game they play.

But, don't you see from the above, how silly it is to look upon me as an impracticable dreamer. I don't claim any particular commercial smartness. But I think I've got ordinary common sense. Facts are facts, and the fact is that I am the only person in the world who has ever sold my books. I sold *Toto, In His Own [Image], Rubaiyat, [Chronicles of the House of] Borgia, Hadrian [the Seventh], [Don] Tarquinio*, all by myself. First wrote 'em: then hawked 'em. No agent ever did a thing. And now the same thing's happened again.

Do you wonder, then, that I shout so confidently '*Oh, give me my goods and my freedom, and see how I'll coin money*'.

For this last offer for *The Weird*, that I will name my own terms, means that I can ask *and have* the usual '*Thousand Pounds cash in advance of a 9d a copy royalty*' by return of post. The publishers know nothing about B. and T. and P-G. The whole thing's absolutely in my hands. I could sign agreement, scoop the money, and give as much or as little of it as I liked to B. and T. and P-G. if I were that kind of person. But I'm not. I'm merely a highly capable kind of person *in more ways than one*, and won't make money for other people for nothing, any longer. That's all.

I did hope you would have written in answer to my last. It is horrible, horrible, never having a friendly word from anyone. Peter has completely disappeared since I last wrote. No one speaks to me now, excepting Barbieri, who comes and curses me because no money has come in. As though that were my fault.

Well he'll turn me out *Aug. 5th or 6th* for certain. So help me if you can. Otherwise I simply can't see how to keep on. And of course I shall have to annul all the work which I've sown so patiently in America. No one shall benefit by it unless I do.   R.

25

August 21, 1910.

Dear F.,

Ten thousand thanks for your last. It has enabled me to go on till now and to get things into something like a definite scheme. I fancy that I have contrived to frighten everybody all round. First of all I have been investigating the stories which Benson[55] used to get me under his priestly thumb before I left England, and before he thought he had tamed me enough to make it safe for him to threaten me with loss of his friendship unless I would implore him to let me write that damned book about Saint Thomas of Canterbury for him to pose as its sole author. The chief of these stories was this. 'Archie Marshall'[56] (who is Alston Rivers the publisher) 'tells me that John Murray[57] is infuriated against you on account of your having made some improper demand for money'; says Benson to me. Of course I said that I didn't know what the devil he meant; I'd never had a row with John Murray who had always treated me decently. And I snorted. 'Let me put it straight: I'm your friend whom you can trust: and I can do it better than you, because you do put people's backs up so when you write letters' says Benson. So I left it to him. And never another word. Of course, *being the shy hypersensitive man I am (though no one believes it)* I felt awfully annoyed to think that nasty things were being said against me. But I obeyed Benson's injunctions to lie low and to trust him to see me righted. Well, having done his best in this sort of way to fill my mind with the idea that I depended on him entirely, he, as I've told you, demanded that I should write that book for him. I refused. And lashed out. Then with the notion of *forcing* me, he joins with Barnard and Taylor persuading them to stop my allowance and to refuse to render my accounts – and he joins with Pirie-Gordon and persuades him that it's quite safe to steal all my things and the manuscripts of *The Weird of the Wanderer* and *Hubert's Arthur*. And he persuades me to send a big bundle of my serial manuscripts to his precious friend Lord Alfred Douglas[58] of 'The Academy' who sticks to them and I never see them again. You see the dodge? Stripped naked, with no means of living and with no work at all to sell, an ordinary man would have caved in; and have begged permission to write that beastly little priest's book on any terms. I didn't. That's all. I've denounced Benson to his archbishop, and to everyone else I can think of, for his attempt to make me write his book, and for his causing me to lose my manuscripts to Lord Alfred Douglas. But I haven't unravelled the whole of his iniquities yet; though I've just got something perfectly lovely about the Murray business. It occurred to me to trace Benson's tale. So I wrote quite nicely to Archie Marshall, explaining what B. had told me, saying that I was of course at a loss to understand it, and asking for particulars. He was touring the world (his wife said); and didn't answer. Then I wrote to Murray straight, saying pretty much the same. And Murray was quite explicit—*he didn't know Archie Marshall from Adam, had never met Benson, had never spoken a word to anyone at all about me, and had nothing whatever against me!*

So that settles Benson. I have told him about it and am making up a second categorical denunciation to his archbishop.

Next, I have got someone in Crickhowel to answer my letters: and this means that I am *explaining Pirie-Gordon's robbery of me in his own neighbourhood*; where I also was known and much liked before I left England. It seems that people there have been made to believe that I mysteriously disappeared two years ago. Well: *now they're going to hear why*, and what the Pirie-Gordons' share in my enforced exile actually has been. In other words, I've managed to get *behind Pirie-Gordon's shield of pompous silence*; and he is wondering what I am going to do.

As for Barnard and Taylor, they also have written – not to the purpose it's true: *but it's something to have made 'em speak after more or less perfect indifference of two years.* I wondered how long they would bear denunciation to Law Society, Publishers' Association, Prudential, Foreign Office, Public Trustee, and in my correspondence and conversation generally, as solicitors who refuse to render accounts of their management – who refuse even to render his own publishers' accounts to their client – who sit tight on his work and property, refusing either to negotiate it or to let him negotiate it – who combine against their client, without his knowledge or consent, with Benson and with Pirie-Gordon, being fully cognisant of each and every iniquity wrought by those two blameless blighters. I know that a man who fancies that people conspire against him is usually thought to be an enthusiast fit for a sanatorium. But – tell me – when solicitors combine in writing (I have the writing) with two men whom they know to have robbed their client, and in their turn refuse him the use of his own creations and property – doesn't the law of England call such combination of spoilers by the unpleasant name of 'Conspiracy'? I think you'll find that it does. Anyhow, Benson, and Pirie-Gordon, and Barnard and Taylor, have begun to have an inkling of what it really is which they've been doing. I think they rather wish that they had not.

Now that is the point at which we have arrived. How to make use of it is the next thing to consider.

Of course it stands to reason that they won't move in a desirable direction, *unless they get a violent shove.* They're desperately uncomfortable where they are: but they know that they're quite safe, because I have neither money nor friends with which to move against them. The perfect hail-storm of annoying (because accusing) letters with which I have flurried them is disagreeable, no doubt:

but they don't look for anything more than letters from me.

But – if I suddenly stopped – if none of them got any more particulars of the sufferings which they have caused me – *then they would have to move.*

And you must also take into consideration at this point, that the life which I lead here becomes day by day more unbearable. The tale of rats which I have trapped in my room amounts to *61*. I am served after the servants. I'm snubbed and insulted by the servants because I can't tip them and because the landlord and his secretary don't even say good morning to me. And so on.

Further, you must know that the Consul has been got at. How, or why, or by whom I don't know. But he has just written *spontaneously* to offer me a passage to Dover or Newhaven, third class and without luggage. It is curious, because he refused my request for that very thing last June twelvemonth when it would have been useful. It is no good now. Indeed it's worse than useless. It would make me look like a fool after my solemn assertions that I wouldn't be driven away. *And besides, I'm just as powerless in England, without friends or money, as I am here. More so, in fact.*

So you see that, strategically speaking, my obvious duty is to say, definitely, to the Consul, and to Barbieri, and to the Benson-Pirie-Gordon-Barnard and Taylor combination, 'I feel it my duty to warn you that I am at the end of my endurance and quite tired out'.

And having said that, I stop writing and calmly go out to live in the open air – somewhere like that lonely part between the Excelsior and Malamocco.

This would throw all these people into each other's arms. The Consul (who got frightened enough over my pneumonia) would want to know where I was, lest he should be accused of ill-treating a British subject. Barbieri would rush to the Consul in a frightful state about the publication of my new book which he depends on for his money, and can't publish without me. And these two would worry B. and T. already worried to death with trying to find out what devilish game my sudden silence was concealing.

The first thing which would be discovered would be that I had, just before disappearing, made my will, had it properly witnessed by the nurses at the hospital and sent it to the Public Trustee as my executor. And that discovery would not be exactly soothing. Would it?

The result – well – there wouldn't be much difficulty about finding me: because I'm not thinking of covering up my tracks, or hiding, or doing anything disgraceful or surreptitious. The Carabinieri of the Lido, as you know, understand that I'm an eccentric English who takes spells of open air for studying for the sake of his writing. We are on the best of terms; and they never interfere with me.

But – what then – when the Consul (pushed to it by an agitated Barbieri, or by no less agitated B. and T.) finds me – what then? Simply this – *I absolutely refuse to listen to anything but an acceptable proposition.* I've said all I have to say. I've urged Pirie-Gordon, and Benson, and B. and T. to give me my work which they've stolen, or at least to let me use it (and I've shewn you that I can sell one book at least, tomorrow, and on my own terms); and now I'm not going to say any more. I've told the Prudential of all the means which B. and T. have used to procure their realisation of my policy. And I've told the Foreign Office of the way in which a British Subject has been robbed and left to die in exile. And I've also arranged for diaries and the complete history of the thing in correspondence to go to the Press in the event of a catastrophe. Therefore, I flatly refuse to listen to anything from the people who have to gain by my *life – not by my death,* now except an acceptable proposition, i.e. *a proposition which will enable me to live in decent peace and comfort and go on with my work.*

BUT, I think it unwise to begin this, unless I am certain of being able to carry it through. One mustn't cry 'Wolf!' It would be fatal and ridiculous to go and live on the Lido shore, if I had to starve there. I don't mind hardship. But it wouldn't do to weaken my body to the extent of weakening my will. And, owing to the police regulations of Italy, a foreigner unpossessed of means of support is instantly expelled beyond the frontier. That wouldn't do at all.

So I say lend me five pounds. With that in my pocket, I fancy I can do the trick. It will take about a month: for that I must be prepared to shift from Malamocco to Pellestrina perhaps. *I must be in a position to defy –* if you understand. If you can manage more, so much the better. The more I have the better and the sooner I can reach a successful conclusion. Do answer *at once.* This is the 'psychological moment'.

Ever yrs, R.

Peter has completely vanished.

Epilogue

Thus ends abruptly the surviving correspondence of Frederick Rolfe with Masson Fox. The springs of charity, it seems, had at last dried up, and no answer ever came to the author's piteous appeal for five pounds. Perhaps by now Fox had begun to feel that the prime causes of Rolfe's troubles lay within himself. It is unlikely, however, that after writing twenty-four times in less than a year, Rolfe would have borne such a state of affairs with equanimity and stopped short without another word.

Of course no real evidence exists to support such a conclusion, yet one cannot but surmise that he followed this letter with others which may have been destroyed. Not to have prodded his patient correspondent still further and finally covered him with abuse would have been utterly out of character.

The reader will perhaps recollect a passage in one of Rolfe's letters (No. 7) where he says:

'Why is it that I have had so many friends in the past, and now have lost them all? The reason is simple. They got tired. They liked me; and they pitied my penury; and they gave me little teaspoonsful of help. But friendship is only possible among equals. There must not be any money mixed up with it. And, by and bye, you also will get tired and bored and annoyed by the continual groans which I'm forced to emit, howling for a strong hand once for all to come along and haul me out of this damned bog and set me on my feet.'

Many were those friends who 'liked' Rolfe and eventually 'got tired' of his unceasing demands for help. But when the time came for the break, they were not to be quit of him without considerable trouble. Nothing he liked better than a good row, and Fox's failure to come to his aid would surely have provided an opportunity to launch at once into the offensive. If this was in fact his last letter to Fox, then the series is unique in one respect, for Rolfe's correspondences with close friends invariably follow a well-defined pattern, ending in violent quarrelling and bitter recriminations.

Notes

1 This is the earliest surviving letter in the correspondence. A postcard, which seems to have preceded it, has apparently been lost.
2 This may refer to Eduardo Bolck, whose name recurs in subsequent letters, notably No. 5.
3 Cockerton, later referred to as Cock and Cocker, was probably a wealthy American friend of Fox who accompanied him on his holiday in Venice. He has not yet been further identified.
4 Rolfe was a member of the Royal Bucintoro Rowing Club in Venice and used its facilities extensively. During periods of homelessness he gave the Club address as his own, and much of his later literary work was done there. There are frequent references to the Bucintoro in his novel *The Desire and Pursuit of the Whole*.
5 This is Bettamio, who is referred to again in letter No. 7.
6 P. is Pietro Venerando, G. is Ermenegildo Vianello, C. is Carlo Caenazzo, and little G. is Giuseppe. In *The Desire and Pursuit of the Whole* Rolfe was to commemorate Gildo as Zildo, who later is revealed as Zilda.
7 It is evident from Rolfe's letter of January 20, 1910, that there is more in this apparently innocent reference than meets the eye.
8 The *lira* at that time was equivalent to 9¾d., or 20 American cents; and 25 *lire* to the £stg, or 5 *lire* to 1 U.S. $.
9 Rolfe was working on his 'romance of modern Venice', *The Desire and Pursuit of the Whole*.
10 Charles Kains Jackson was a City solicitor and journalist. He edited *The Artist* and was the moving force behind *The Chameleon*, which figured prominently in the trials of Oscar Wilde. In *The Quest for Corvo* Symons describes Jackson's first meeting (and subsequent friendship) with Rolfe which occurred at Gleeson White's house in Christchurch during the early Nineties. The letter quoted by Symons (op. cit., pp. 26–27), in which Rolfe refers to Jackson, was addressed to their mutual friend J. G. F. Nicholson (see footnote 23, below).
11 This was Charles Francis Cazenove, a director of the Literary Agency of London, founded in 1899. Rolfe is known to have sent a number of MSS to him at the end of September 1909, but the agent was unable to place them. There is no record of the Literary Agency's failure.
12 His host from August 1909 until March 1910 was the resident English doctor, Ernest van Someren. The fullest account of Rolfe's eight months at the van Somerens' is contained in Victor Hall's illuminating article 'The Last Years: Some Memories of Rolfe in Venice, Recalled by Mrs Ivy van Someren, in an Interview' (*Corvo 1860–1960*, St Albert's Press, 1961). According to Mr Hall, Rolfe was 'treated as one of the family, and the complaints made by him in his correspondence about "the poor table" and "unconvivial atmosphere" had no basis in fact. . . . His contribution to the household consisted chiefly of chopping and carrying logs for a large boiler and working a cream separator. When he was not performing these tasks he confined himself to his room, writing for many hours a day.' The doctor is described by Mr Hall as 'a most charitable man, well-known in Venice for his Christian efforts to help those in trouble.' He founded the Cosmopolitan Hospital, which Rolfe attacked so bitterly in *The Desire and Pursuit of the Whole*, and where, when the author contracted pneumonia the following year, he was taken for treatment. Despite what Rolfe

says in this letter, he was to spend a further four and a half months as the van Somerens' guest.

13 Henry Scott Tuke, R.A., R.W.S., an English artist who enjoyed a great vogue during the Nineties and the early years of this century. Like Fox he was a Quaker and lived in Falmouth. His work was not remarkable for originality of design or vigour of construction. He concentrated on the special artistic problem of the treatment of nude flesh in sunlight, his models being nearly always boys, though he occasionally painted a female figure. He is represented in the Tate Gallery by two of his most important pictures: 'August Blue', representing four boys bathing from a boat, and 'All Hands to the Pumps', one of his few grey subjects. In the biography of the painter by his sister, Maria Tuke Sainsbury, it is recorded that in about 1890 Tuke sent some drawings to Rolfe, 'perhaps to help him in' the murals on which he was then engaged. 'Rolfe was too fantastic a man to attract [Tuke] much,' according to Mrs Sainsbury.

14 Rolfe was an artist of some versatility. After his rejection from the priesthood and before turning to literature he worked intermittently as a painter. Few of his pictures have survived, but the processional banners he painted for St Winefride's, Holywell, are still in existence.

15 (Sir) Frank Brangwyn, R.A., the English decorative painter, practised nearly all the visual arts and crafts, from architecture to book illustration. One example of his work in architecture is the British Pavilion for use at the Biennial Exhibition in the Public Gardens at Venice. At the time when Rolfe was writing Brangwyn was the one living English artist of whom any foreigner had heard and his prestige in this country was correspondingly great. He executed commissions from all over the world. During his later years he lived at Ditchling, in the settlement of Roman Catholic artists and craft workers.

16 Augustus Montalba and his four spinster sisters were English by birth and had settled many years earlier in Venice. Each of the Montalba sisters was in her own way a gifted artist, the most successful being Clara. She was a frequent exhibitor at the Royal Academy and her work was widely known on the Continent.

17 Giuseppe Miti Zanetti, an Italian painter, etcher and lithographer of some repute in his time. Born in Modena, Miti Zanetti settled in Venice as a young man and the result was a succession of land- and sea-scapes depicting that city, many of which possess a remarkable lyrical quality.

18 Leslie Antill & Skeels, sometime of Basinghall Street in the City of London; solicitors.

19 Barnard & Taylor, of Lincoln's Inn Fields, solicitors, represented Rolfe in his legal action against Colonel Owen Thomas. Rolfe claimed that he had 'ghosted' for Thomas a book entitled *Agricultural and Pastoral Prospects of South Africa*. The case was heard in January 1907 and the verdict was given against Rolfe. Between 1904 and 1908 Barnard & Taylor advanced Rolfe some £600, in return for which the author assigned to them the rights in various literary works and also a life insurance policy. When, in October 1908, the solicitors refused to allow him any further funds he quarrelled with them; and the present reference is to one of the many attempts which Rolfe made to redeem the rights in his work. It was not until 1912 that he found the 'financial partner' willing to take over his assets and liabilities from Barnard & Taylor and to make him an allowance. This was the Rev. Justus Stephen Serjeant, who appears in *The Quest for Corvo* as 'Stephen Justin'.

20 These were Rolfe's novel *Don Renato* and the translation into English prose, made in collaboration with Sholto Douglas, of the Greek Anthology songs of

Meleager, both of which were to have been published in London by Francis Griffiths. *Don Renato* had already been printed and bound and *Meleager* was in the early stages of production; but, as a result of Rolfe's embargo, they were destined to remain unpublished till 1963 and 1937, respectively.

21 Rolfe's account of the incident that follows recurs in the twenty-sixth chapter of *The Desire and Pursuit of the Whole*, on which he was then engaged.

22 The reference is, I think, to the mythical but extensively quoted friend of Mrs Gamp, in Dickens's *Martin Chuzzlewit*.

23 John Gambril Nicholson was a schoolmaster and the author of a volume of one-act plays, two novels and four collections of verse. He appears first to have met Rolfe while he was a pupil at Saffron Walden Grammar School where Rolfe was a master. Nicholson's verses show marked technical facility, but otherwise have little merit. Both he and Tuke shared an obsession with adolescent boys; Nicholson's books and Tuke's paintings are full of it.

24 Rolfe first met Harry Pirie-Gordon at Oxford in 1905 while he was acting as secretary and amanuensis to the Vice Principal of Jesus College, Dr E. G. Hardy, and Pirie-Gordon was keeping a post-graduate year devoted to history. A friendship was at once formed, and during the next three years Rolfe was to spend much time at Pirie-Gordon's home in Breconshire. Among the fruits of this association were the two collaborated novels, *The Weird of the Wanderer* and *Hubert's Arthur*. It is scarcely necessary to say that the accusations which Rolfe makes against Pirie-Gordon and Barnard & Taylor are for the most part malicious distortions of the truth.

25 Frank Victor Rushforth (born *c*. 1890), had met Nicholson in about 1902. He was a member of Caius College, Cambridge, where, in 1909, he took the Wesleyan Lay Preachers' Examination. He went out to India the following year and is believed to have died there shortly afterwards.

26 Edward Carpenter, English writer, social reformer and pioneer of a return to rural simplicity. Earlier in the year Rolfe had begun writing a counter-blast to Carpenter's long prose-poem *Towards Democracy* under the title *Towards Aristocracy*.

27 The reference is to Nicholson's *Love in Earnest* (1892) which included a sonnet, composed originally by Rolfe and revised by Nicholson, entitled 'St William of Norwich (Painted by F. W. Rolfe).' After the book was published Rolfe threatened the author with legal action, with the result that the publishers were obliged to remove from unsold copies the leaf containing the plagiarized sonnet.

28 Cockerton and Charles Kains Jackson.

29 Castelfranco Veneto, a town and episcopal see of Venetia, in the province of Treviso.

30 November 28th.

31 The bridge of St Eufemia is on the Giudecca waterfront, facing the Zattere.

32 This expression is used by Rolfe to mean that he rewarded P[eter], C[arlo], Z[ildo] and others of the clan.

33 Campo San Polo. After Piazza San Marco this is the largest square in Venice. Palazzo Mocenigo Corner, a beautiful work of 1548, by Michele Sammichele, is No. 2128.

34 December 11th.

35 The van Somerens moved later in 1910 to Palazzo da Mula, S. Vio, on the Grand Canal, and subsequently to Calle Cicogna 2406, Via Ventidue Marzo, in the San Marco quarter.

36 One of the two Rolfe had in mind was John Markoleone, the Jewish boy

whom he had met in Bristol the previous year. He describes this boy in some detail in his correspondence with Professor Dawkins. He refers to him again on page 45 of this collection.

37 Harold Frederic, American journalist and novelist. *Illumination* (1896) was a clever character study, showing the effect upon a simple, pious Free Church minister of an introduction to a new world of culture, art and beauty. The book had a great success both in Britain and America.

38 Although Fox appears to have made fairly frequent contributions to Rolfe's finances, the sums which are acknowledged, other than this 'wired 50', are rarely more than a pound. We may reasonably conclude that the 50 were *lire* and not pounds. Rolfe's reference earlier in this letter to 'the way you chuck it about' may well contain an element of mild sarcasm. It is noteworthy that in his final letter Rolfe asks Fox to send him five pounds, a request to which his correspondent apparently failed to accede.

39 This was the address of the Hotel Belle Vue. It was here, at the north-east corner of the Piazza, that Rolfe had stayed from his arrival in Venice with Professor Dawkins, early in August 1908, till April 14, 1909, when, unable to settle his account, he was evicted. In his next letter, dated April 5, 1910, Rolfe writes that 'the landlord of the Bellevue has taken the *Clock Tower in the Piazza*' and 'given me an empty attic here to sleep in.'

40 *The Desire and Pursuit of the Whole*. The serialization to which Rolfe refers did not take place.

41 *The Weird of the Wanderer: Being the Papyrus Records of Some Incidents in One of the Previous Lives of Mr Nicholas Crabbe, Here Reproduced by Prospero & Caliban*, was one of two novels composed by Harry Pirie-Gordon which were taken over and entirely rewritten by Rolfe. The 'English' firm from whom Rolfe received the offer was William Rider & Son Ltd, who published the book in 1912.

42 This is possibly a reference to Rolfe's lost novel *Sebastian Archer*, the plot of which he describes in chapter fifteen of *The Desire and Pursuit of the Whole*.

43 (Countess) Marie Tarnowska was a notorious Russian seductress who was tried in Venice during March and April 1910 for unsuccessfully persuading one of her lovers to murder another.

44 I am unable to elucidate the significance of this opening, unless it refers to a photograph which was enclosed with the letter and has since perished.

45 Evaristo Barbieri, the proprietor of the Hotel Belle Vue.

46 Rolfe frequently refers to *Nicholas Crabbe* and *The One and the Many* as two separate books. If he contemplated a work with the separate title of *The One and The Many*, it was never written. This is the subtitle, however, of *Nicholas Crabbe*, which was destined to remain unpublished till 1958.

47 Victor Emmanuel III. Sir Shane Leslie states in his article 'Frederick Baron Corvo' (*The London Mercury*, September 1923) that 'Rolfe worked out an elaborate pedigree to show that Victor Emmanuel was the rightful King of England, to whom, as his rightful sovereign, copies of his books were formally presented.'

48 Herbert Rolfe, characterized by Symons in *The Quest for Corvo* as 'the reluctant brother'.

49 That is, the Armenian Benedictines on the island of San Lazarro, near the Lido, one of the many religious communities in Venice where Rolfe might possibly have availed himself of the traditional hospitality.

50 This island adjoins the Public Gardens, at the eastern extremity of Venice.

51 Barnard & Taylor, solicitors.

52 In a letter to Harry Pirie-Gordon dated November 7, 1909, Rolfe had demanded the manuscripts of *The Weird of the Wanderer* and *Hubert's Arthur*, the 'two finished' books referred to, and *The King of the Wood*, *The Burrowers*, and 'the unnamed MS. about the Boy-Popes Benedict and John'. These last three works were never completed and the MSS are lost. What the fourth 'half-finished' book was, I am unable to determine.

53 Solfatara di Pozzuoli is the crater of a half-extinct volcano situated in the volcanic region between Naples and Cumae. The country still abounds in hot mineral springs, *fumarole* (fissures from which vapours and sulphurous gases ascend) and funnel-shaped craters containing hot mud.

54 In fact fate was more merciful to him than Rolfe prophesied, for Peter was later to serve in the *carabinieri*, marry, and live to a ripe old age.

55 (Mgr) Robert Hugh Benson, Catholic novelist and apologist. His tempestuous friendship with Rolfe, beginning in 1905; their period of collaboration on a novel based on the life of Thomas à Becket which was later abandoned; and the cooling off and subsequent termination in their relations are described by Symons in chapter fourteen of *The Quest for Corvo*. Benson's methods of breaking with Rolfe over the proposed book have never reflected much to his credit. His biographer glosses over the whole episode.

56 Arthur Hammond Marshall, who wrote under the name of Archibald Marshall, was well known as a novelist and contributor to *Punch*.

57 (Sir) John Murray, the fourth head of the famous London publishing house. His grandfather, John the second, was the friend of Byron, Moore and Scott.

58 (Lord) Alfred (Bruce) Douglas, the poet and close friend of Oscar Wilde. He was the proprietor and editor of *The Academy*, which published Rolfe's short story 'Deinon to Thely'.